THE
RIGHTS OF
PRISONERS

THE AMERICAN CIVIL LIBERTIES UNION HANDBOOK SERIES

AN AMERICAN
CIVIL LIBERTIES
UNION HANDBOOK

THE
RIGHTS OF
PRISONERS
THE BASIC ACLU
GUIDE TO A
PRISONER'S RIGHTS

David Rudovsky

General Editors of this series:
Norman Dorsen, *General Counsel*
Aryeh Neier, *Executive Director*

 **Richard W. Baron
New York**

To those prisoners who, despite the fear of
retaliation, continue to struggle to change
our dehumanizing prison system.

Acknowledgments

I would like to express my appreciation to Eve
Cary of the New York Civil Liberties Union,
Kitzi Burkhart, Muffin Friedman, and Mark Williams for their comments and suggestions which
were extremely useful in writing this book.

Contents

Preface

This guide sets forth your rights under present law and offers suggestions on how you can protect your rights. It is one of a series of guidebooks published in cooperation with the American Civil Liberties Union on the rights of teachers, servicemen, mental patients, prisoners, students, criminal suspects, women, and the very poor.

The hope surrounding these publications is that Americans informed of their rights will be encouraged to exercise them. Through their exercise, rights are given life. If they are rarely used, they may be forgotten and violations may become routine.

This guide offers no assurances that your rights will be respected. The laws may change and, in some of the subjects covered in these pages, they change quite rapidly. An effort has been made to note those parts of the law where movement is taking place but it is not always possible to predict accurately when the law *will* change.

Even if the laws remain the same, interpretations of them by courts and administrative officials often vary. In a federal system such as ours, there is a built-in problem of the differences between state and federal law, not to speak of the confusion of the differences from state to state. In addition, there are wide variations in the ways in which particular courts and administrative officials will interpret the same law at any given moment.

If you encounter what you consider to be a specific abuse of your rights you should seek legal assistance. There are a number of agencies that may help you, among them ACLU affiliate offices, but bear in mind that the ACLU is a limited-purpose organization. In many communities, there are federally funded legal service offices which provide assistance to poor persons who cannot afford the costs of legal representation. In general, the rights that the ACLU defends are freedom of inquiry and expression; due process of law; equal protection of the laws; and privacy. The authors in this series have discussed other rights in these books (even though they sometimes fall outside the ACLU's usual concern) in order to provide as much guidance as possible.

These books have been planned as guides for the people directly affected: therefore the question and answer format. In some of these areas there are more detailed works available for "experts." These guides seek to raise the largest issues and inform the non-specialist of the basic law on the subject. The authors of the books are themselves specialists who understand the need for information at "street level."

No attorney can be an expert in every part of the law. If you encounter a specific legal problem in an area discussed in one of these guidebooks, show the book to your attorney. Of course, he will not be able to rely *exclusively* on the guidebook to provide you with adequate representation. But if he hasn't had a great deal of experience in the specific area, the guidebook can provide some helpful suggestions on how to proceed.

Norman Dorsen, General Counsel
American Civil Liberties Union

Aryeh Neier, Executive Director
American Civil Liberties Union

Introduction

As an institution, our penal and "correctional" system is an abject failure. The conditions in America's jails and prisons virtually ensure psychological impairment and physical deterioration for thousands of men and women each year. Reformation and rehabilitation is the rhetoric; systematic dehumanization is the reality. Public attention is directed only sporadically toward the subhuman conditions that prevail in these institutions, and usually only because the prisoners themselves have risked many more years in confinement, and in some cases even their lives, to dramatize their situation by protest. Attica was but one example of an undercurrent of tension, hatred, and hostility that threatens to rip apart the uneasy rule by fear which prevails in most penal institutions today.

Have there always been prisons?
No. It was not until the nineteenth century that the use of prisons became widespread. Until the middle of the eighteenth century, European penology was motivated principally by punishment and retribution. Most crimes were dealt with by corporal punishment and a great many by execution. Imprisonment was thought to be a deterrent

11

to criminal activity (an idea prevalent today although still
not established through objective criteria) and was considered more humane than corporal punishment. Moreover,
prisons were also built with the idea of reformation: the
penitentiary was intended to serve as a place for reflection
in solitude leading to repentance and redemption. But these
prisons served in reality only to punish—physically and
mentally. Supported by court-adopted theories that prisoners were in fact slaves of the state, prison administrators
had absolutely free reign to abuse their inmates as they
wished. There was no question of prisoners' "rights."

Didn't the courts rule on prison conditions?

No. The courts concurred in the notion that incarceration in prison was for punishment and adopted a "hands-
off" policy which prevented prisoners from securing any
rights except those their jailers allowed. Few persons, including lawyers, attempted to challenge this policy. This
abdication of judicial responsibility reinforced the status
quo of prison life and, because no other political or social
institutions responded to the prisoners' complaints, the
penal system became isolated from public scrutiny.

The practical effect of the "hands-off" policy was to
place all decisions concerning internal affairs of the prison
within the discretion of the prison officials, no matter how
arbitrary and inhumane the results. The courts continually
deferred to the so-called expertise of the prison administration in refusing even to hear complaints by prisoners concerning violations of their most fundamental rights.

Do courts today rule on prison conditions?

Yes. The "hands-off" policy is now slowly being replaced by a judicial attitude that seeks to eliminate the major abuses suffered by prisoners. But despite substantial legal victories over the past decade, the prisoners' lot has improved, practically speaking, only with respect to major abuses and severe physical punishment. The erosion of the hands-off doctrine has hardly resulted in judicial activism. Even liberal courts have failed to confront what one commentator has correctly termed the "central evil" of prison life—"the unreviewed administrative discretion granted to the poorly trained personnel who deal directly with prisoners."[1] Moreover, even those rights which are now guaranteed by the courts are often illusory for many prisoners. Implementation and enforcement of these rights rest primarily in the hands of prison officials who continue to fight for the status quo. Litigation is costly and time-consuming, and few lawyers have volunteered their service in this area. Thus even those minimal rights which appear on paper are often in reality denied.

On what principles do courts rely in deciding prisoner-rights' cases?

Generally, courts rely on three principles. First, that lawful incarceration necessarily deprives a prisoner of certain rights and privileges he would enjoy in the free society; second, that a convict does not lose all of his civil rights—certain fundamental rights follow him (with appropriate limitations) through the prison gates, and are to be protected by the courts; finally, that prison officials are vested with wide discretion and unless constitutional or other fundamental rights are involved, the federal courts are reluctant to interfere with internal operations of prison discipline.[2]

This formulation of the federal courts' role in protecting prisoners' rights is sufficiently broad and contradictory that, given virtually any set of facts, a court could deny or give relief relying on one or more of the principles stated. In some cases more specific rules have been announced by the courts, but we are still far from a concise and predictable rule of law in prisons. In one of the most perceptive and enlightened opinions discussing the general constitutional framework in which prisoner-rights' suits should be decided, a federal district court reasoned:

> In my view, in passing upon . . . challenges to the rules for institutional survival [censorship, body searches, summary procedures in disciplinary hearings, etc.], the balance must be struck in favor of the individual rights of the prisoners. That is to say, if one of these rules of institutional survival affects significantly a liberty which is clearly protected among the general population, and if its only justification is that the prison cannot survive without it, then it may well be that the Constitution requires that the prison be modified. Specifically, if the functions of deterrence and rehabilitation cannot be performed in a prison without the imposition of a restrictive regime not reasonably related to those functions, it may well be that those functions can no longer be performed constitutionally in a prison setting. Also, with respect to the comparatively few offenders who simply must be physically restrained for periods of

time to prevent them from committing antisocial acts, it may well be that the society will be compelled, constitutionally, to allocate sufficient resources for physical facilities and manpower to permit this function of physical restraint to be performed in a setting which little resembles today's prisons.[8]

Why have courts consistently refused to look behind the decisions of prison administrators and merely deferred to their "expertise"?

It is the answer to this question that provides an important key to understanding prison life. Judges have known for years that many prison rules and procedures are irrational, inhumane, and illegal, but they have used the "hands-off" doctrine, in effect, to avoid discussion of these problems. The obvious result is that prison officials are left with total control over the prisoners in their institutions. Of course, the more unchecked, the more arbitrary, and the more capricious the power of a prison administrator, the easier it is for him to rule. The political judgment that a "hands-off" policy indicates is, quite simply, that prisoners may be abused in whatever way their keepers desire, for this will ensure order and control in a system that is virtually bankrupt of any positive values or norms.

Who runs the prison system?

The prison system in America is an extremely diverse collection of facilities, techniques, and programs. The hundreds of thousands of commitments each year are dispersed to town, city, county, state, and federal institu-

tions which range from the overnight lockup for the drunk
or disorderly to maximum-security blocks for the long-
term inmate. Each level of government operates inde-
pendently of the others in administering its prisons and
correctional apparatus. Thus, the Federal Government
has no control over state corrections; the states have
responsibility for prisons but usually no control over
county or city jails; and the rules and regulations vary
substantially from penal institution to penal institution.

What law applies to prisons?

The only source of law applicable to all prisons is the
Constitution, which provides only a minimum standard for
prisoners' rights.

Ideally, state and federal statutes, and administrative
rules and regulations could expand these rights, but except
in a few instances, the Constitution continues to provide
the most meaningful basis for assertion of prisoners' rights.
Most state statutes vest almost complete power and discretion for rule-making in prisons to an administrative Bureau
of Corrections or similar board. The regulations established by these agencies rarely guarantee any significant
rights for prisoners and most often only generally provide
rules for the maintenance of security in the prison. For
these reasons, most of the rights now guaranteed to
prisoners are a result of judicial rulings rather than legislative or administrative action.

This does not mean, however, that in the assertion of
prisoners' rights, the statutes and rules of the prisons should
be ignored. Indeed, unless prison administrators begin to
change their attitudes and policies, no number of constitutional decisions will cause a perceptible change. These

"paper rights" must be upheld and enforced and that duty and power remains in the hands of prison officials.

The discussion of substantive rights that follows in the next several chapters applies fairly generally to all prisoners in the United States, but while some of these rights are now secure for all prisoners, many others are provided only in some states or federal circuits and not in others. Wherever possible the breakdown among different jurisdictions is indicated.

Are there many court decisions in the area of prisoners' rights?

No. Compared to most legal areas the number of decisions involving prisoners' rights is small, reflecting not only the very recent change in the attitude of the courts concerning their responsibility to ensure the constitutional rights of prisoners, but also the harsh reality that only a few prisoners have the resources and courage to challenge the actions of their jailers in the courts.

The relatively small number of cases discussed, while representative of the types of complaints that prisoners have, does not accurately represent the number of prisoners who are daily denied their constitutional rights. Even now, as the knowledge of rights grows among prisoners, the court dockets show a marked increase in prisoner-rights' cases. Whether the courts will meet this challenge and establish a rule of law for prisons consistent with the Constitution remains to be seen. If they do not, however, we should not expect that prisoners will agree to continue suffering under inhumane conditions for they, too, understand the politics and dynamics of our penal system. If

legal relief is not provided, other, less-peaceful attempts
at securing rights will surely follow.

NOTES

1. Hirschkop, "The Rights of Prisoners," in *The Rights of Americans,* 451, N. Dorsen, ed. (1970).
2. See, *e.g., Courtney v. Bishop,* 409 F.2d 1185 (8th Cir. 1969).
3. *Morales v. Schmidt,* 340 F.Supp. 544 (W.D.Wisc. 1972).

I

Due Process

Do prisoners have a right to due process at prison disciplinary proceedings?

Prisoners traditionally have been given few, if any, of the rights normally guaranteed by the due-process clause. Prison administrators have always had total power to make rules, usually vague and unwritten; enforce them, usually inconsistently; and arbitrarily prescribe punishment. Recently the issue of prisoners' due-process rights at disciplinary proceedings has been taken up in the courts. This is important because disciplinary proceedings affect a large number of prisoners and can result in serious consequences including loss of all rights and privileges (visits, reading material, recreation), placement in solitary confinement, and denial of parole.

How are prison disciplinary proceedings run?

Disciplinary proceedings are usually initiated upon a complaint of a guard or other prison official that a prisoner has violated a prison rule or regulation. The matter is then

19

referred to the prison disciplinary committee ("adjustment committee," "prison board," and so on) for disposition. This committee is composed of high prison officials such as the warden, associate warden, classification officers, and others.

From here, the process differs from state to state and institution to institution. In some, the committee will reach a decision on the complaint and summarily order punishment. The decision is made solely on the complaint and any other information that the committee may have concerning the incident and the inmate's background. More often the procedure followed is to conduct a "hearing" at which the committee or disciplinary board meets with the prisoner, notifies him of the charges, and allows him an opportunity to respond. However, the complaining guard is not present and cannot be cross-examined; the inmate is not represented by counsel or a counsel-substitute and is not allowed to call witnesses on his own behalf. Moreover, the committee often considers material in the inmate's file other than that which is relevant to the case (past charges, prior conduct, and so forth in the prison), and decides the case on an overall view of the inmate's conduct in prison rather than on the relevant facts pertaining to the charge against him. Only in isolated cases have prison officials granted prisoners who are charged with disciplinary infractions more procedural protections, such as the right to call witnesses, to cross-examine the prison guard, and to be represented by counsel or counsel-substitute.

What are the possible results of a disciplinary proceeding?

Various forms of dispositions and punishment can be ordered as a result of these hearings. In some cases the "charge" will be dismissed and no change in status will occur. Available statistics indicate, however, that in most cases some form of punishment is ordered. For institutional offenses, the punishment may take the form of revocation of prison privileges for a certain period of time; short-term placement in segregation; involuntary transfer to another penal institution (usually one that has a higher form of security); loss of accumulated good time and, most ominously, referral of the disciplinary finding to the parole board for its consideration upon an inmate's application for release on parole.

Which due process rights are prisoners entitled to at disciplinary hearings?

Courts have rarely specified the due process rights required at disciplinary hearings although some have found prison regulations too restrictive of an inmate's right to be heard and have ordered changes in hearing procedure. The Second Circuit Court of Appeals, for example, ruled that the facts in a prison disciplinary proceeding must be "rationally determined" and the prisoner should be "afforded a reasonable opportunity to explain his actions,"[1] but it refused to specify procedural rights, implicitly rejecting claims for cross-examination of prison officials, right to counsel, and the right to present witnesses on the inmate's behalf. Other courts similarly have held that the "relevant facts must not be capriciously or unreliably determined"[2] and that "sufficient safeguards" must be provided where the possible punishment is "sufficiently great."[3]

A few courts have been more precise. In California a federal district court held that prior to any administrative punitive action a prisoner must be given written notice of the charges against him; a record of the hearing; the right to cross-examine witnesses against him and to call witnesses on his own behalf; the right to counsel and to have counsel appointed if he is indigent; a decision in writing setting forth the reasons for the decision, the evidence upon which it is based and the legal basis for the punishment imposed.[4]

A federal district court in Virginia ruled in 1971 that where disciplinary proceedings may result in the loss of substantial rights, the prisoner accused has the right to retain counsel or a lay advisor, to cross-examine witnesses against him, and to call witnesses in support of his defense. The court found that the state had no substantial interest in summary adjudication and held that minimum due-process rights must therefore be afforded.[5]

In a Rhode Island case, a federal district court ordered the adoption of various regulations concerning classification of prisoners and transfers for punitive reasons. This ruling followed a canvass of the prison population by the court and should end the practice of prison administrators of buying off the rights of prisoners by threatened transfer to punitive segregation or denial of other rights.[6]

Unless these decisions are followed disciplinary hearings will continue to be run like "kangaroo courts," causing deep resentment among prisoners.

Is there any precedent for granting due process safeguards at prison disciplinary hearings?

Yes. In extending the due process rights of prisoners, the courts have had substantial precedent to rely upon. The procedural due process rights now being requested by inmates go no further than those already secured by numerous persons in this country who face loss of a right or a privilege through administrative action. The courts have required due process rights to welfare recipients who face loss of their welfare payments,[7] to government employees faced with the possible revocation of security clearance,[8] to students who face expulsion from a university,[9] and to citizens who merely seek to obtain a state liquor license or whose good name or reputation is at stake as a result of a state law which allows bars to list the names of persons who should not be served.[10]

Certainly, the substantial deprivations that may result from prison disciplinary proceedings are as serious as those just mentioned and should not be imposed without at least the rudimentary protection that due process is meant to ensure. There can be a sliding scale of due process safeguards that could be determined by the severity of the possible punishment. The principle that should guide application of due process is that the greater the potential impact of a disciplinary decision on the conditions of present or prospective liberty, or the physical and psychic integrity of the prisoner, the greater the need for procedural safeguards.[11]

Are there established regulations governing inmates' rights and responsibilities in prison?

No. Few prisons provide their inmates with adequate notice of what conduct is considered illegal. A short orientation is sometimes provided outlining the general duties and responsibilities of prisoners, but they do not even begin to detail the various rules and regulations, the violation of which will result in disciplinary citations. Moreover, where regulations do exist, they are usually extremely vague and subject to definition on an ad hoc basic by the enforcing officials.

Without a set of written rules and regulations, enforcement of discipline in the prison will, by definition, always be arbitrary and capricious, for a most fundamental notion of the rule of law is prior notice of what in fact is deemed by authorities to be illegal.

Who decides what conduct is illegal?

The prison guards. The present system puts absolute discretion and day-to-day power over every aspect of a prisoner's life in their hands. It is this part of prison life which causes the deepest resentment among prisoners for, to a large extent, the manner in which an inmate is treated by the guards determines the severity of conditions he will have to endure. It is a double irony that the lower the level of authority in prison (from warden on down to guard) the greater the discretion that is vested in the prison official and the less willing the courts are to review their decisions. Thus, whether it be a request for medical treatment, the right to go to the yard or prison library, or the potentially more serious matter of prison discipline and punishment, the guard on the block holds ultimate power over the prisoner. Complete discretion in the context of prison life, where no remedies exist to correct it, can be catastrophic. Judge Soberloff has put it bluntly:

> In fact, prison guards may be more vulnerable to the corrupting influence of unchecked authority than most people. It is well known that prisons are operated on minimum budgets and that poor salaries and working conditions make it difficult to attract high-calibre personnel. Moreover, the "training" of the officers in dealing with obstreperous prisoners is but a euphemism in most states.[12]

An inmate at Holmesburg Prison in Philadelphia understated the problem when he testified that physical brutality was not the major problem in prison. It was instead "the problem . . . that the guard doesn't realize how important his authority is" and that the resentment among prisoners is most clearly traceable to the guards manifesting an attitude in which the prisoner is regarded as "something less than a human being."

How can arbitrary treatment of inmates by prison authorities be curbed?

Prison officials should be ordered to establish written rules and regulations to govern institutional conduct. These should limit as far as possible the discretion of guards and other prison personnel in regulating prisoner conduct. As

in the free society, where no rules or regulations forbid a
certain kind of conduct, no punishment should be allowed
for its exercise. To date, the right to this type of rule of
law has not been generally recognized by the courts. In
fact, very few cases have presented this question for direct
resolution. It must be recognized, however, that written
regulations defining the rights and responsibilities of
prisoners, placing limitations on possible punishment, and
limiting the power and discretion of prison officials is the
minimum that is required by due process of law.

Have any courts acted to control arbitrary acts by prison officials?

Yes. Recent decisions by federal district courts recognize
the serious due process problems posed when prison rules
fail to provide adequate advance notice of what conduct
on the part of prisoners can result in discipline and punishment. In Louisiana, a federal court ruled that prison
authorities must officially promulgate rules and regulations
which will adequately apprise the prisoner of what conduct can subject him to serious discipline, what penalty
he can expect, and the procedure by which such a determination will be made. The court further required that a
copy of these rules and regulations be furnished to each
inmate.[13]

In Virginia, the federal court recognized the fact that
few decisions have ever dealt with this problem, but felt
compelled to require the prison to establish specific written
rules governing prisoners' conduct.[14] This was necessary
to allow prisoners to conform to the rules and to prevent
prison administrators from imposing arbitrary penalties.
The abundance of vague regulations (prohibiting, for ex-

ample, misbehavior, misconduct, and agitation) persuaded
the court that these regulations offered no reasonable
guidance to inmates, and left administrators free to apply
subjective standards in judging conduct and imposing
punishment. Accordingly, the prison officials were ordered
to file with the court a list of rules and regulations concerning standards of behavior and a schedule of minimum
and maximum punishments for their violation.

In New York, a federal district court ruled that the
posting of rules in the first-floor receiving room of The
Tombs (Manhattan House of Detention) was not sufficient
notice to prisoners of what conduct on their part would
be considered illegal. The court required prison officials
to adopt a comprehensive set of rules, to be approved by
the court, governing inmate behavior, lock-out times and
procedures, use of commissary, chapel, medical services,
and other important aspects of inmate life. These rules
would be set out in a booklet given to each new prisoner.[15]

In the most expansive opinion and order concerning the
need for notice of fair prison regulations, a Maryland
state court has ordered that Patuxent Institution in Maryland adopt an exhaustively detailed code of rules and
regulations written by the court at the suggestion of the
inmates' counsel.[16] The court listed conduct which would
constitute offenses subject to institutional sanctions and
detailed the kind of punishment that could be imposed for
each offense, limiting confinement in solitary to a maximum
of fifteen days. In addition, a code was promulgated governing disciplinary hearings and providing for full due process
protections, including the right to counsel and appeal.

NOTES

1. *Sostre v. McGinnis,* 442 F.2d 178 (2d Cir. 1971).
2. *United States ex rel Campbell v. Pate,* 401 F.2d 55, 57 (7th Cir. 1968).
3. *Nolan v. Scafati,* 430 F.2d 548 (1st Cir. 1970).
4. *Clutchette v. Procunier,* 328 F.Supp. 767 (N.D. Cal. 1971).
5. *Landman v. Royster,* 333 F.Supp. 621 (E.D. Va. 1971); See also *McCray v. Maryland,* 10 Cr. L. Rptr. 2132 (Md. Cir. Ct., November, 1971).
6. *Morris v. Travisono,* 310 F.Supp. 857 (D.R.I. 1970); See also, *Krause v. Schmidt,* 341 F.Supp. 1001 (W.D. Wisc. 1972).
7. *Goldberg v. Kelly,* 397 U.S. 254 (1970).
8. *Greene v. McElroy,* 360 U.S. 474 (1960).
9. *Dixon v. Alabama State Board of Education,* 294 F.2d 150 (5th Cir. 1961).
10. *Wisconsin v. Constantineau,* 400 U.S. 433 (1971).
11. See *Wisconsin v. Constantineau,* 400 U.S. 433, 436 (1971). Justice Douglas stated: "It is significant that most of the provisions of the Bill of Rights are procedural, for it is procedure that marks much of the difference between rule of law and rule by fiat."
12. *Landman v. Peyton,* 370 F.2d 135, 140 (4th Cir. 1966).
13. *Sinclair v. Henderson,* 331 F.Supp. 1123 (E.D. La. 1971).
14. *Landman v. Royster, supra.*
15. *Rhem v. McGrath,* 326 F.Supp. 681 (S.D.N.Y. 1971).
16. *McCray v. Maryland, supra.*

II

Freedom from Cruel And Unusual Punishment

Prisoners have an absolute right to be free from cruel and unusual punishment under the Eighth Amendment, but while it is an easy matter to state the basic right, it is extremely difficult for prisoners to persuade the courts to act when faced with anything less than barbaric prison conditions.

Historically, the Eighth Amendment's ban on cruel and unusual punishment was aimed at preventing a recurrence of torture and barbarous punishments common in England and colonial America such as disembowling and decapitation. During the nineteenth century, this provision was thought to be virtually obsolete as these punishments were no longer imposed. In 1910, however, the Supreme Court gave added force to the Eighth Amendment, holding that the Amendment's protections were not tied to a particular theory or point in time.[1]

The Eighth Amendment rests upon fundamental considerations of human decency: it has been held to contain a "basic prohibition against inhuman treatment" and its basic underlying concept "is nothing less than the dignity of man." The amendment was designed to assure that the state's punishing power be exercised within the limits of civilized standards, and it "must draw its meaning from the evolving standards of decency that mark the progress of a maturing society."[2] An 1892 Supreme Court decision provides the touchstone for the amendment's application to conditions in prisons. It held that the government is ". . . bound to protect against lawless violence all persons in their service or custody in the course of the administration of justice."[3]

What constitutes cruel and unusual punishment?

At present there appear to be three principal tests that are applied under the Eighth Amendment: (1) whether the punishment shocks the general conscience of a civilized society; (2) whether the punishment is unnecessarily cruel; and (3) whether the punishment goes beyond legitimate penal aims.

The first and second standards would, if applied, substantially correct the major overt physical abuses of prison life. The third asks a basic question which goes beyond prison regulations and policy: Is this restriction of a prisoner's rights necessary?

The problem is, in a sense, one of burdens of proof. If the prison officials are compelled to justify their restrictive policies as other government officials must when basic constitutional rights are asserted by citizens, many of the policies would be declared unconstitutional. But if courts continue to accept prison administrative policies on the grounds that courts lack the expertise to review these matters, little besides the gross abuses of prison life will be ameliorated.

What conditions in prisons amount to cruel and unusual punishment?

A leading case involving prisoners' rights under the Eighth Amendment is *Holt v. Sarver*[4] concerning conditions of institutional life within the Arkansas penitentiary system. The court undertook an extensive review of all of the alleged unconstitutional practices at the prisons and held that the cumulative impact of the substandard conditions constituted a system of cruel and unusual punishment. Chief Judge Henley stated:

> The distinguishing aspects of Arkansas penitentiary life must be considered together. One cannot consider separately a trustee system, a system in which men are confined together in large numbers in open barracks, bad conditions in the isolation cells, or an absence of a meaningful program of rehabilitation. All of those things exist in combination; each affects the other; and taken together they have a cumulative impact on the inmates regardless of their status.

Specifically, the court found that the open-barracks system and the use of trustee guards rendered confinement "inherently dangerous" and violative of the inmates' rights to be free from cruel and unusual punishment. The court stated: "A convict, however cooperative and inoffensive he may be, has no assurance whatever that he will not be killed, seriously injured, or sexually abused. Under the present system the state cannot protect him." In making

this assessment the court took into consideration the history
of physical attacks in the prison, the lack of a rehabilitative
program, inadequate medical facilities, unsanitary conditions in the cells and kitchen, the lack of an adequate
classification system, and the racial segregation of facilities.
It found that while some of these conditions, considered
individually, might not constitute a violation of the Eighth
Amendment, their cumulative and interrelated effect was
significant and, therefore, was an integral part of the
"overall constitutional equation before the Court."

In reaching its decision the court stated:

> For the ordinary convict a sentence to the Arkansas
> Penitentiary today amounts to a banishment from
> civilized society to a dark and evil world completely
> alien to the free world, a world that is administered
> by criminals under unwritten rules and customs com-
> pletely foreign to free-world culture.
>
> Apart from physical danger, confinement in the Peni-
> tentiary involves living under degrading and disgust-
> ing conditions. This Court has no patience with those
> who still say, even when they ought to know better,
> that to change those conditions will convert the prison
> into a country club; the Court has not heard any of
> those people volunteer to spend a few days and nights
> at either Tucker or Cummins incognito.[5]

Other courts have adopted this approach. The Pennsylvania Supreme Court ruled that the general conditions
prevailing in a Philadelphia prison (including overcrowded, wet, and infested cells, improper classification of prisoners, insufficient medical treatment, and ran-
dom physical beatings by guards) rendered confinement
there cruel and unusual punishment even though the pris-

oners who complained were not themselves beaten, sexually attacked, or suffering the most serious abuses of the prison. The court held that the mere fact that they were subject to these conditions was a sufficient showing of unconstitutionality.[6] Courts in Detroit, Michigan,[7] Lucas County, Ohio,[8] and Gallup, New Mexico,[9] have similarly ruled that confinement in local jails amounted to cruel and unusual punishment. In West Virginia, however, a court has refused to release inmates despite evidence of inmate murders, forced homosexuality, a kitchen described as irredeemably unsanitary, and censorship of all communications. This, the court reasoned, did not amount to cruel and unusual punishment.[10]

Is solitary confinement cruel and unusual punishment?

It can be. A claim of cruel and unusual punishment need not be based on the totality of prison life. It may also be established by reference to a particular condition of confinement. It should surprise no one that most cases raising the issue of cruel and unusual punishment concern confinement in segregation, strip-cells, or solitary. No court has ruled that confinement in segregation or solitary confinement is cruel and unusual punishment per se. To the contrary, numerous cases around the country have upheld the use of solitary confinement. However, the courts have drawn limits as to what kinds of physical conditions and treatment may be tolerated. As a federal district court in California stated:

> When, as it appears in the case at bar, the responsible prison authorities in the use of the "strip cells" have abandoned elemental concepts of decency by permit-

ting conditions to prevail of a shocking and debased nature, then the court must intervene . . . to restore the primal rules of a civilized community in accord with the mandate of the Constitution of the United States.[11]

The conditions that moved the court to act were compelling:

During his eleven-day confinement in a 6′ by 8′4″ "strip cell," he was not adequately protected from the wet weather; he was deprived of all items by which he might maintain bodily cleanliness; he was forced to eat the meager prison fare in the stench and filth caused by his own vomit and body wastes; he could wash his hands only once every five days; and he was required to sleep naked on a stiff canvas mat placed directly on the cold concrete floor.[12]

Other cases in which courts have declared conditions in solitary to be cruel and unusual include the following: In a Tennessee prison, the inmate was placed in a five-foot by eight-foot cell, unlighted, and made to sleep nude on the floor. There was only a hole in the floor for his wastes and the flushing of this matter was controlled by a guard outside the cell.[13]

In Arkansas, the federal courts have ruled, in several cases, that where solitary confinement is in dirty, overcrowded, venemous cells, without proper ventilation, limited opportunity for exercise and dirty food, the proscription against cruel and unusual punishment is violated.[14]

A New York federal court has ruled that conditions in solitary confinement in state prisons were cruel and unusual where the complaining inmates were kept nude; had only a blanket on the bare floor on which to sleep; had no light, radio, or smoking privileges; had to stand all day; and had only a toilet and washbowl, but no toilet paper in the cell.[15] The court said:

> We are of the view that civilized standards of humane decency simply do not permit a man for a substantial period of time to be denuded and exposed to the bitter cold . . . and to be deprived of the basic elements of hygiene such as soap and toilet paper.[16]

But, in Texas, a federal court upheld solitary confinement, where the prison provided a wash basin, drinking fountain, steel bunk without a mattress, blanket, cloth gown, toothbrush and a shower every other day, even though the cell was kept in complete darkness and the daily diet was bread and water with a "full" meal every seventy-two hours.[17]

Are there any restrictions on the imposition of solitary confinement?

Yes. Solitary confinement may also be cruel and unusual where the reason for isolation or the length of incarceration in isolation is not justified by the alleged violation of prison regulations, even though the physical conditions do not fall below the standards required by the Eighth Amendment. Thus, a federal district court in Washington, D.C., has ruled that isolation in solitary confinement for two years constituted cruel and unusual punishment because the only violation of prison rules—engaging in a demonstration tending to breach the peace—was relatively minor.[18]

In an important New York case involving Martin Sostre, the lower court had held that confinement in the "primitive segregation" unit of a New York prison for more than fifteen days was cruel and unusual punishment no matter how serious the infraction of prison regulations. However, the Court of Appeals reversed this ruling, holding that the conditions in solitary at the prison—including a diet which was basically the same as that given to the general prison population, the availability of at least rudimentary implements of personal hygiene, the opportunity for exercise, and the provision of some reading material—were not so barbaric or inhumane as to justify a blanket proscription against confinement there for over fifteen days. The court, however, left undecided the question of whether confinement of one year in solitary could be justified for fewer or less serious charges, thus indicating that a prisoner has a right not to be confined in solitary for an excessive period of time.[19]

Similarly, a federal court in Pennsylvania has held that if the circumstances are sufficiently serious to warrant long-term isolation, confinement in solitary for four hundred days is not per se unconstitutional.[20]

Have any specific punishments been held to be cruel and unusual?

Yes. The courts are beginning to establish minimal requirements for individual aspects of confinement in solitary. As a result, it now appears that inmates have a right to a reasonable opportunity for physical exercise. In Georgia, a federal district court has held that there was no constitutionally acceptable justification for denying segregated prisoners a chance to exercise[21] and a federal district court in Louisiana ruled that where an inmate on death row was allowed out of his small cell for only fifteen minutes a day in which time he must bathe, exercise, and wash clothes, the constitutional proscription against cruel and unusual punishment was violated. The court held that confinement for long periods of time without the opportunity for regular outdoor exercise violates the Eighth Amendment.[22]

In Virginia, a federal district court has enjoined the practice of providing only bread and water to prisoners. Noting that such a diet provides a daily intake of only seven hundred calories compared to the average need of two thousand calories for sedentary men, and taking judicial notice that such a diet is deficient as well with respect to other necessary dietary elements, the court concluded that the resultant pangs of hunger constitute a dull, prolonged sort of corporal punishment.[23]

Crowding of prisoners in isolation also came under scrutiny. Acknowledging that overcrowding, per se, may not be violative of the Eighth Amendment, the court nevertheless enjoined extended, unnecessary confinement in substandard solitary cells of more men than the cell was meant to hold.

Is corporal punishment allowed in prisons?

No. Most states by regulation forbid the imposition of corporal punishment. And the Court of Appeals for the Eighth Circuit has ruled, in enjoining the use of the strap (for whipping), that any form of corporal punishment is cruel and unusual punishment within the meaning of the Constitution.[24]

The Virginia Federal Court also invalidated several other facets of punishment that had been used in the Virginia state prisons. First, the practice of controlling misbehavior by placing inmates in chains or handcuffs in their cells was held unjustified since the result of such punishment was, in various cases, the infliction of permanent scars, lack of sleep, and prolonged physical pain. In addition, the court prohibited officials from taking away inmates' clothing unless a doctor states in writing that the inmate's health will not thereby be affected and that the inmate presents a substantial risk of injuring himself (or herself) if given garments. The use of tear gas was also enjoined. It was pointed out that prison officials had other, far less drastic means available for enforcing discipline in the prison.[25]

Is sexual deprivation considered cruel and unusual?

No. The denial of conjugal visits presents an important question with respect to the prohibition against cruel and unusual punishment. Heterosexual deprivation, of course, is the rule in virtually every prison in this country. This condition causes anxieties and aggression, frustrates rehabilitation, and disrupts family relationships. Nevertheless, most people accept this enforced abstinence as a legitimate part of prison life and it has never been held to be cruel and unusual punishment. Only the state of Mississippi allows conjugal visits, although Pennsylvania, California, Iowa, and Louisiana now provide for furloughs on a limited basis. In this area, our correctional system falls far behind those of thirty other countries which allow furloughs and conjugal visits.

NOTES

1. *Weems v. United States,* 217 U.S. 349 (1910).
2. *Trop v. Dulles,* 356 U.S. 86, 100-101 (1958); *Weems v. United States, supra.* See also, *Furman v. Georgia,* 408 U.S. 238 (1972) (imposition of capital punishment under discretionary statutes constitutes cruel and unusual punishment).
3. *Logan v. United States,* 144 U.S. 263 (1892).
4. 309 F.Supp. 362 (E.D. Ark. 1970), *aff'd* 442 F.2d 304 (8th Cir. 1971).
5. *Id.* at 381.
6. *Commonwealth ex rel. Bryant v. Hendrick,* 444 Pa. 83 (1971) (court ordered two inmates released upon writ of habeas corpus).
7. *Wayne County Jail Inmates v. Wayne County Board of Commissioners,* C.A. No. 173-217 Cir. Ct. Michigan, March 25, 1971.
8. *Jones v. Wittenberg,* 323 F. Supp. 93 (N.D. Ohio, 1971).
9. *United States ex rel. Curley v. Gonzales* (Nos. 8372-73, D.N.M., 1970).
10. *Pingley v. Coiner,* 10 Cr. L. 2367 (January 25, 1972, W.Va. Supt. Ct. App.).
11. *Jordan v. Fitzharris,* 257 F.Supp. 674 (N.D. Calif. 1966).
12. *Id.* at 680.
13. *Hancock v. Avery,* 301 F.Supp. 786 (M.D. Tenn. 1969).
14. *Holt v. Sarver, supra.*
15. *Wright v. McMann,* 387 F.2d 519 (2nd Cir. 1967).
16. *Id.* at 526.
17. *Novak v. Beto,* 453 F.2d 661 (5th Cir. 1971).
18. *Fulwood v. Clemmer,* 206 F. Supp. 370 (D.C.D.C. 1962).
19. *Sostre v. McGinnis,* 442 F.2d 178 (2nd Cir. 1971).
20. *Knuckles v. Prasse,* 302 F. Supp. 1036 (E.D. Pa. 1969), aff'd, 435 F.2d 1255 (3d Cir. 1970).
21. *Krist v. Smith,* 309 F.Supp. 497 (S.D. Ga. 1970).

22. *Sinclair v. Henderson*, 331 F.Supp. 1123 (E.D. La. 1971).
23. *Landman v. Royster*, 333 F.Supp. 621 (E.D. Va. 1971).
24. *Jackson v. Bishop*, 404 F.2d 571 (8th Cir. 1968).
25. *Landman v. Royster, supra.*

III

Free Communication and Access to the Courts—The Problems of Prison Censorship

Do prisoners have the right to freedom of communication?

The law is unclear on this issue. Court decisions are quite contradictory and, therefore, of limited use in advising prisoners of their rights to free communication. The older cases tend to uphold almost all forms of prison censorship; more recent decisions have tended to restrict the use of censorship and, in conjunction with liberalized administrative rules and policies governing censorship, have established for many prisoners a right to freer communications with the outside world than existed years ago. This is particularly true with respect to communications with attorneys, the courts, and government officials. However, limitations on correspondence and reading materials

41

are still prevalent, primarily because old shibboleths concerning the "need" for censorship remain unexamined by the courts.

Do prisoners have the right to correspond with their lawyers and the courts?

Yes. The greatest degree of protection thus far afforded to prisoners' correspondence has been with courts, counsel, and government officials. In one of the few cases that the United States Supreme Court has directly ruled on an issue concerning prisoners' rights, *Ex Parte Hull*,[1] the court struck down a prison regulation providing that all legal documents, prior to being forwarded to a court, were subject to a prison official's determination as to whether they were properly drawn. This regulation was held to be an abridgment on the right to petition a federal court for a writ of habeas corpus. In so holding, the court indicated that the question of whether a writ was proper in form or substance was for the courts to determine; it was not a matter for a decision by a prison official.

Following this decision, one would expect that prison administrators and the courts would not only protect the right of prisoners to have reasonable access to the courts, but would protect as well the right to confidential communciations with counsel and government officials. Nevertheless, prisoners still do not have the absolute right to communicate freely with the courts, their attorneys, or government officials. Most prisons continue to screen and read all outgoing and incoming mail and some prisons censor these communications (that is, either delete sections of communications or fail to deliver the entire letter).

Do prison authorities have the power to interfere with an inmate's legal correspondence?

The power to open, read, and censor prisoners' legal mail has been substantially limited by the federal courts; and significant opinions have resulted from cases in Rhode Island,[2] New York,[3] and Ohio.[4]

The opinion by the Rhode Island court is of particular significance because it is one of the few cases which analyzes, challenges, and ultimately rejects the rationale behind prison censorship. First, in a sweeping review of jail-censorship policies, the court observed that total censorship serves no rational deterrent, rehabilitative, or prison-security purpose. Judge Pettine held that it was unconstitutional to censor any letters that criticize jail conditions since this was one of the only vehicles available to prisoners to inform the public about prison conditions. The court also ruled that the prison had no right to "protect" the public from vulgar or insulting letters from prisoners.

Second, the court held that prison officials may not open or inspect outgoing *or* incoming mail to or from the courts, attorneys, or a long list of government officials. In fact, Judge Pettine has required by his decision that prison officials obtain a search-and-seizure warrant *prior* to reading any outgoing mail. This, of course, properly places the burden on prison officials to obtain judicial approval of any interference of outgoing mail based on the Fourth Amendment's requirement that probable cause exist to believe that evidence of a crime will be uncovered in the mail.

With respect to incoming mail, the court ruled that all letters (except those from counsel, the courts, and the government officials) may be inspected for drugs, weapons, and contraband, and may be read to detect and censor hard-core pornography and highly inflammatory writings. However, under the court's order, if any mail or other material is censored or confiscated, prison officials must notify the prisoner to whom the mail was addressed.

The New York Court of Appeals has held that prison officials have no right to open, read, or inspect mail to and from the courts, but ruled, on the other hand, that the prison officials could constitutionally censor mail between prisoners and attorneys unless the correspondence concerned complaints of unlawful treatment.[5]

A federal district court in Massachusetts has ordered that any censorship or interference with correspondence between an inmate and his attorney is violative of the inmate's First Amendment rights. The court reasoned that the exclusion of contraband could be secured by use of a fluoroscope, a metal detection device, or by manual manipulation of the envelope.[6] Similarly, a federal court in Maine has ruled that while the prison may open incoming mail from attorneys to check for contraband, the opening must be done in the presence of the inmate.[7]

In *Sostre v. McGinnis*,[8] the Second Circuit Court of Appeals in 1971 ruled that a prison may not delete, withhold, or refuse to mail communications to courts—even when the communications are irrelevant to the prisoner's case or even false and malicious—unless it is determined that the prisoner is "abusing" his rights by communicating about "restricted matters." However, to aid prison officials in determining such "abuses" the court has allowed prison officials in its jurisdiction the full right to open and read *all* outgoing and incoming correspondence.

Some prison administrators now permit uncensored communications between prisoners and the courts. In federal prisons, inmates are permitted to send sealed, uncensored letters to any judge, attorney general, senator, or similar official. Similarly, some states, including California and Pennsylvania, now allow free communications of this nature.

May prisoners correspond with legal-assistance agencies?

Yes. Several courts have upheld the right of prisoners to correspond with legal assistance agencies like the American Civil Liberties Union and with lawyers they had not previously retained on the ground that reasonable access to the courts is predicated, at least in some situations, on an opportunity to interest attorneys in taking the prisoner's case. At least one federal court, the Court of Appeals for the Eighth Circuit, stipulated that prison officials may place reasonable restrictions on correspondence with the ACLU.[9] And in a somewhat analogous context, the Fourth Circuit Court of Appeals permitted a prisoner to write to *Playboy* magazine in an effort to raise money for his defense, but somewhat characteristically and without stating any reasons, the court added the proviso that his letters must not be critical of the prison administration.[10]

An important decision in this area has resulted from the efforts of inmates at Green Haven Prison in New York to organize a Prisoners' Labor Union. See pp. 76-77. Several prisoners had written to the Prisoners' Rights Project of the New York Legal Aid Society requesting advice and assistance with respect to the formation of the Union. Prison officials refused to recognize the Union and withheld letters from the Legal Aid Society to prisoners at Green Haven. The Second Circuit Court of Appeals ordered the officials to deliver the letters, holding that they did not present a clear and present danger to the security of the institution. The court stated:

> Under the test for attorney-client mail, the state must show clearly an abuse of access in order to justify restriction. Defendants claim that such an abuse exists here, because the letter advocated an "unlawful scheme," one instance mentioned by the *Sostre* court in which some restriction would be permissible. The contention that an application for recognition of the Union and communication with one's clients preparatory to such application are components of an unlawful scheme seems a misuse of that term. The lawyers were telling the prisoners to utilize lawful, not unlawful channels for the presentation of grievances and were guiding a challenge to a prison rule through orderly procedures. It is difficult to discern in what other fashion the prison would prefer to have the rule examined; it is the only peaceful method by which it can be reviewed by someone other than the Commissioner or his deputy, who are naturally interested in quelling any inmate activity which may arrogate to inmates themselves some decision-making power about the conditions of prison life.[11]

What procedures are used in censoring prisoners' mail?
Prison censorship procedures are by their very nature arbitrary. In most prisons, censorship is conducted by guards or other custodial personnel. As a rule, there are no regulations to guide their determinations as to what

should be censored, and if guidelines do exist they are so vague as to leave complete discretion in the censoring official. Not only does this lead to extreme variations from guard to guard as to what mail is censored, but it provides the guard with an additional unreviewable power to arbitrarily govern and punish prisoners.

Moreover, prisoners are very rarely informed that their mail (either incoming or outgoing) has been withheld or censored, thus effectively denying them any opportunity to challenge the guard's action. Often, by the time the prisoner realizes that his mail has been censored, it is too late to complain to higher officials in the prison.

Wouldn't uncensored correspondence create a security risk in a prison?

No. The claim by administrators that censorship is necessary, even with respect to communications with the courts and legal counsel, rests on the theory that the mails might be used to transmit contraband, to plan escapes, or to engage in other unlawful schemes. The likelihood of any of these dire predictions becoming reality is very slim indeed. The experience in jurisdictions which permit an unlimited right to communication indicates that there is, in fact, no support for these fears. And since most prisons allow confidential visits between counsel and prisoners, there is no need to use the mails to organize these illegal schemes. It should be the duty of the correspondent (the court, government officials) to report any illegal activity, and contraband in incoming mail can hardly be said to be a primary concern when the mail comes from the courts, lawyers, or government officials. Certainly, in view of the importance of the attorney-client relationship and the due process right of access to the courts, the minimal chance of abuse of the right to free communications is certainly outweighed by the constitutional rights of the prisoners that are involved.

Why shouldn't a prison official have a right to read a prisoner's mail?

Because it is an unnecessary intrusion on the prisoner's right to privacy. And, as importantly, because prisoners would be unable to report bad conditions to people on the outside. Prisoners are often "punished" in one of the numerous low-visibility ways that prison officials employ in dealing with unpopular or rebellious prisoners when their communications consist of complaints to courts concerning prison conditions or actions of prison officials. Often, this punishment involves only an exercise of discretion and therefore cannot be a successful basis for any legal challenge to the official actions. Second, it may very well deter other prisoners from exercising their right to communicate with the courts. If there is a fear that such communications will result in some form of retribution, it is likely that at least some prisoners will not risk the consequences. Several courts have held it to be unconstitutional for prison officials to impose or threaten to impose punishment based upon a prisoner's complaints to a court.[12]

Do prisoners have the right to correspond with anyone other than lawyers, courts, and government officials?

Correspondence with individuals other than court personnel, lawyers, and government officials is almost always subject to censorship and other restrictions. Typically, a prison will maintain an approved list of correspondents for each prisoner. This list is usually limited to persons having a "legitimate" relationship to the inmate—for example, famliy and one or two friends—and prison regulations often limit both the number of correspondents a prisoner may have and the number of letters he may send out per day. The Rhode Island court that has greatly expanded prisoners' right to free communications has at the same time upheld a prison regulation limiting correspondence, aside from mail to attorneys, religious figures, or government officials, to one letter per day.[13]

Is non-legal correspondence censored?

All non-legal letters may be read. Frequently, they are then censored. Regulations usually provide that letters may not be offensive to race, nationality, or religious faith; that they may not criticize the rules, regulations, or officials of the prison; that they not be "sexually arousing" (many prisons return mail smelling of perfume!); and that they not discuss matters that do not directly and personally concern the prisoner.

Courts have rarely come to grips with the substantial First Amendment problem posed by this type of censorship. In one case, a prisoner had been punished for criticizing prison officials in a letter to his parents. The federal court rejected the prison's predictable assertion that the punishment was necessary to aid in the rehabilitation of the prisoner, stating that rehabilitation is not "abject acceptance of all prison conditions, however unjustifiable." It broadened its previously stated rule, protecting the right of prisoners to complain to the courts about prison conditions, to include complaints to private persons. Moreover, the court invoked a First Amendment analysis that is sadly lacking in many other cases:

> Any prison regulation or practice which restricts the right of free expression that a prisoner would have enjoyed if he had not been imprisoned must be related both reasonably . . . and necessarily, . . . to the advancement of some justifiable purpose of imprisonment. . . . A prisoner could be punished only if he acted or threatened to act in a way that breached or constituted a clear and present danger of breaching the justifiable regulation.[14]

Do prisoners have a right of access to the media?

Yes. In the past year, prisoners have been making a determined effort to air their grievances through the media. In pursuit of this goal, they have attempted to secure the right to send letters to the press which are critical of institutional policies and treatment. The United States Court of Appeals for the First Circuit has recently vindicated that right with an opinion that lays to rest many of the arguments for censorship.[15] The court held that prisoners have a right to send letters to the press concerning prison management, treatment of offenders, or personal grievances except those which (1) contain or concern contraband, or (2) contain or concern any plan of escape or device for evading prison regulations. The court found that the need for this right is "buttressed by the invisibility of prisons to the press and the public; the prisoners' right to speak is enhanced by the right of the public to hear." Under this ruling, prison officials may continue to open and read these communications, but only to determine if the inmate was adhering to the court's limitations.

In a precedent-setting decision a federal court has ruled that the policy of the Federal Bureau of Prisons prohibiting any interviews between prisoners and news reporters violates the First Amendment.[16] The court held that newspapers should have the right to interview willing inmates not only because prisoners are constitutionally entitled to have their views and complaints made public through the media, but, in addition, because:

> Prisons are public institutions. The conduct of these institutions is a matter of public concern. Whenever people are incarcerated, whether it be in a prison, an insane asylum, or an institution such as those for the senile and retarded, opportunity for human indignities and administrative insensitivity exists. Those thus deprived of freedom live out of the public's view. It is largely only through the media that a failure in a particular institution to adhere to minimum standards of human dignity can be exposed. Indeed, needed reforms in these areas have often been sparked by press attention. Conversely, secrecy is inconsistent with responsible official conduct of public institutions for it creates suspicion, rumor, indifference, if not distrust. Disinterest causes abuses to multiply.

In related developments, the correctional departments of New York, Pennsylvania, and Massachusetts now permit newsmen access to the prisons to interview willing prisoners and a state court in Maryland has ordered that such access be provided, subject to reasonable prison regulations as to time, place, and manner.[17]

Do prisoners have a right to read what they choose?

Despite some advances in recent years, prison officials continue to exercise a heavy hand of censorship on the kinds of books, magazines, and other reading materials that prisoners may possess and read. In some states, prisons maintain a list of approved publications for inmates, while in others the decision as to what books and magazines are legitimate is made on an ad hoc basis. Typically, controversial political, religious, or social books and documents are censored and only reading matter of the most innocuous nature is permitted.

Cases challenging these overly restrictive policies have succeeded only where the courts have agreed to employ the judicial test of "clear and present danger" to determine whether prison discipline or security will be undermined by allowing inmates to read and possess the material in question. The "clear and present danger" test, which governs official attempts to limit First Amendment activity in the free world, places the burden on the prison officials to demonstrate a compelling state interest centering around prison security or prison discipline *prior* to any censorship. Under this standard, much of what has traditionally been censored has now been cleared by some courts.

The Fifth Circuit Court of Appeals, in a case challenging Florida prison policies, which severely limited the right of black prisoners to receive black-oriented papers and magazines, ruled that such policies denied black prisoners their rights under the First Amendment and their right to equal protection of the laws.[18] Black prisoners were given the right to receive *Ebony* and *Sepia* magazines and at least one non-subversive Negro newspaper of their choice.

In 1966, the Fourth Circuit Court of Appeals similarly upheld the right of black inmates to receive black-oriented newspapers.[19]

A federal district court in New York, employing the same constitutional analysis, has ordered that New York State prisoners have the right to receive *Fortune News*, the newsletter of the Fortune Society, an organization of former inmates which publishes articles and information on prison alternatives, ex-convicts' rehabilitation, and other related activities.[20] The court found that the mere assertions that the newsletter did not accurately reflect conditions in the prisons failed to show a compelling reason why it should be banned. In a sharp rebuke to those who would justify censorship in this context, Judge Weinfeld stated:

> Free discussion of the problems of society is a cardinal principal of Americanism—it is part of our cherished heritage. Prison administration has been the subject of deep concern in contemporary society. Citizens, public groups, and officials, as well as inmates, have been sharply critical of our correctional and penal practices and procedures. Various sectors of the community have charged correctional and prison administrators, and the courts as well, with administrative deficiencies and policies. Whether justified or not, prime responsibility for these alleged shortcomings has been attributed by many, including newspapers, to the courts and prison administrators. However distasteful or annoyed or sensitive those criticized may be by what they consider unfair criticism, half truths or information, it does not justify a ban of the publication carrying the alleged offending comments. Censorship is utterly foreign to our way of life; it smacks of dictatorship. Correctional and prison authorities, no less than

the courts, are not above criticism, and certainly they possess no power of censorship simply because they have the power of prison discipline.

In a similar decision, another federal district court in New York has permitted Black Panther prisoners to receive and read the Panther newspaper despite the court's own adverse reaction to its content.[21]

Martin Sostre, an outspoken black prisoner in New York, has litigated several facets of the "right-to-read" issue. The Second Circuit Court of Appeals held that he could not be punished for possessing "inflammatory" and "racist" literature, but made it clear that he had no right to distribute the material to other prisoners.[22]

The district court in New York has partially vindicated Sostre's rights in another case in the receipt-of-literature area. State prison officials had withheld issues of the Black Panther newspaper, the *Workers World,* and several books including the writings of Mao Tse-tung. At the time this material was withheld, no regulations existed to guide prison officials in determining whether to censor reading material. Nor were prisoners provided the right to contest these decisions. The court ruled that reading material could only be withheld if it posed a clear and present danger to the security of a prison or to the rehabilitation of prisoners, and further required that prior to censorship the prisoner must be notified of the intent to censor, be given some opportunity to object to the censorship, and be provided with a decision by an impartial board applying constitutional standards.[23]

Do prisoners have a right to publish their own writing?

Restrictions exist also on an inmate's right to disseminate and publish his own written materials outside the prison. For example, the Federal Bureau of Prisons requires submission of all manuscripts to the warden prior to publication on the outside. This regulation has been upheld by a federal court in Connecticut in a case involving Daniel and Phillip Berrigan, who had attempted to bypass the rule by sending sermons directly to outside contacts. The court rejected the argument that this regulation was an invalid restriction of their right under the First Amendment.[24]

In an unusual case, the California Supreme Court has ruled that prisoners who write books that are published while they are incarcerated cannot be forced to contribute any part of their royalties to the prison administration.[25] The charge supposedly was for "handling costs," but the court found that prison censors were compensated by the state and that the prisoner-author was not benefited by this payment in any respect.

In a related area, the courts have also upheld prison regulations that make written communications between prisoners subject to seizure and censorship. The rationale is the same as that given for most prison censorship—the need to protect against escape attempts and other illegal plans.[26]

May prison authorities prohibit inmates from providing legal assistance to each other?

No. One of the most critical needs of a prisoner who has been convicted and sentenced is competent legal assistance if he desires to challenge his commitment. While the Constitution requires that counsel be appointed for those who cannot retain private lawyers, this right applies only to trials and direct appeals. Most states do not provide free counsel for inmates who institute post-conviction proceedings, that is, attacks on their convictions and sentences after, or in place of, direct appeals. Prisoners are generally provided little or no guidance in determining whether they have grounds for a legal challenge, in preparing writs and in litigating their cases. As a result, the practice of jailhouse lawyering has become widespread with some inmates providing counseling and drafting services for other prisoners.

Up until 1969, prisoners were punished for providing legal assistance to their fellow inmates. Then, in *Johnson v. Avery*,[27] the United States Supreme Court ruled that unless prison officials provide reasonable legal assistance to inmates, they may not prohibit prisoners from assisting each other with legal work. The court found that the due-process right to unimpeded access to the courts overrode any objection that prison officials made on the ground that jailhouse lawyers would interfere with prison discipline.

Do any legal-assistance programs exist?

Many prisons have moved to implement the Supreme Court's directive by establishing legal-assistance programs. These vary from prison to prison, but generally incorporate the use of lawyers or law students to counsel and represent inmates in post-conviction proceedings. Where such programs have not been instituted, courts have invalidated regulations prohibiting "legal practice" by jailhouse lawyers.

In one case, where prisoners showed that the backlog

of requests for legal assistance was so great that they had to wait for eighteen months to receive assistance from law students, the court permitted jailhouse counseling by inmates to continue.[28]

At the state correctional institution at Graterford in Pennsylvania, inmates, with the approval of prison officials, have started a para-professional law clinic to provide legal assistance to inmates. Composed of experienced "writ-writers," with some assistance from legal organizations, the clinic members study transcripts, undertake legal research, and write legal briefs. No compensation of any kind may be accepted by any prisoner.

Other programs designed to meet the Supreme Court's mandate involve combinations of legal services programs, volunteer lawyer assistance, and law-student research and assistance, although student aid alone is not sufficient to satisfy the rights of inmates.

Are there any restrictions on jailhouse lawyers?

Notwithstanding the Supreme Court's ruling, some courts have upheld limitations on the jailhouse lawyer. First, the courts have rejected attacks on regulations that prohibit inmates from soliciting legal business, and from demanding or receiving compensation for their services. This is based on the fact that prison officials have expressed concern that it is the general practice for prison lawyers to demand payment, whether it be in the form of cigarettes, money, or sexual favors, for their services and that by establishing a powerful subculture in the prison, they tend to undermine prison discipline.

Second, the courts have ruled that prisons may limit the time and place of jailhouse lawyering so as to prevent interruption of normal prison activities, so long as the right to counsel is not unreasonably impeded. Furthermore, regulations that place complete discretion in any prison official to permit or prohibit inmate legal assistance at his option are clearly invalid.

Many prisons, even after the Supreme Court ruling, prohibited inmates from possessing another inmate's legal materials or papers in his cell, prohibited the use of typewriters, limited the number of legal books in the prison library and in individual cells, and limited the amount of paper and other material needed for effective legal representation.[29] However, the Supreme Court of California has ruled that inmates may possess legal papers of other inmates since this was integral to effective counseling.[30] The court suggested that the prison had other ways of controlling abuses that may accompany the possession of other inmates' papers. Courts have generally upheld what they have considered to be reasonable limitations on paper, pens, pencils, and legal materials in cells on the ground that they did not unduly interfere with counseling.

As with other court decisions sustaining censorship and restrictions on the kind and quantity of reading material for prisoners, these cases barely touched upon the competing interests of the prison and the prisoners and accepted without analysis the judgment of prison officials that such restrictions were necessary to maintain proper discipline.

The United States Supreme Court has recently placed many of these restrictions in question by requiring California to greatly expand its prison law libraries.[31] The High Court affirmed a lower court's decision holding that:

> A prisoner should know the rules concerning venue, jurisdiction, exhaustion of remedies, and proper parties respondent. He should know which facts are legally significant, and merit presentation to the court, and

which are irrelevant and confusing. . . . "Access to the courts," then, is a larger concept than that put forward by the State. It encompasses all the means a defendant or petitioner might require to get a fair hearing from the judiciary on all charges brought against him or grievances alleged by him.

The lower court also held that "writ-writers" could work and keep legal materials in their cells, but could not permanently store them there. Even the existence of a complete law library does not, of course, afford most prisoners an opportunity to challenge their convictions equal to that of inmates who are represented by counsel. Prisoners need complete legal services for each of their complaints, whether it be with respect to convictions or prison conditions.

NOTES

1. 312 U.S. 546 (1946).
2. *Palmigiano v. Travisono*, 317 F.Supp. 776 (D.R.I. 1970).
3. *Rhem v. McGrath*, 326 F.Supp. 681 (S.D.N.Y. 1971).
4. *Jones v. Wittenberg*, 330 F.Supp. 707 (N.D. Ohio 1971).
5. *Brabson v. Wilkins*, 19 N.Y. 2d 433, 227 N.E. 2d 383 (1967).
6. *Marsh v. Moore*, 325 F.Supp. 392 (D.Mass. 1971).
7. *Smith v. Robbins*, 328 F.Supp. 162 (D.Maine 1971), *aff'd* 454 F.2d 696 (1st Cir. 1972).
8. 442 F.2d 170 (2d Cir. 1971).
9. *Burns v. Swenson*, 430 F.2d 771 (8th Cir. 1970).
10. *McDonough v. Director of Patuxent*, 429 F.2d 1189 (4th Cir. 1970).
11. *Goodwin v. Oswald*, 462 F.2d 1237 (2d Cir. 1972).
12. See, *e.g.*, *Carothers v. Follette*, 314 F.Supp. 1014 (S.D.N.Y. 1970).

13. *Palmigiano v. Travisono, supra.*
14. *Carothers v. Follette, supra;* see also, *Morales v. Schmidt,* 340 F.Supp. 544 (W.D.Wisc. 1972) (prisoner given right to correspond with sister-in-law despite their prior illicit relationship).
15. *Nolan v. Fitzpatrick,* 451 F.2d 545 (1st Cir. 1971).
16. *Washington Post v. Kleindienst,* 1 Prison L. Rptr. 141, _____ F.Supp. _____ (D.D.C. 1972). The court's order has been stayed by the Supreme Court pending the Government's appeal. 92 S.Ct. 1761 (1972).
17. *McCray v. Maryland, supra.*
18. *Jackson v. Godwin,* 400 F.2d 529 (5th Cir. 1968).
19. *Rivers v. Royster,* 360 F.2d 593 (4th Cir. 1966).
20. *Fortune Society v. McGinnis,* 319 F.Supp. 901 (S.D.N.Y. 1970).
21. *Shakur v. McGrath,* 69 Civ. 4493 (S.D.N.Y. Dec. 31, 1969).
22. *Sostre v. McGinnis,* 442 F.2d 178 (2d Cir. 1971).
23. *Sostre v. Otis,* 330 F.Supp. 941 (S.D.N.Y. 1971).
24. *Berrigan v. Norton,* 322 F.Supp. 46 (D.Conn. 1971).
25. *In re Van Gelden,* 97 Cal. Rptr. 698, 489 P.2d 578 (1971).
26. See, *e.g., Denson v. United States,* 424 F.2d 329 (10th Cir. 1970).
27. 393 U.S. 483 (1969).
28. *Williams v. Department of Justice,* 433 F.2d 958 (5th Cir. 1970).
29. See, *e.g., Conklin v. Wainwright,* 424 F.2d 516 (5th Cir. 1970); *McKinney v. Debord,* 324 F.Supp. 928 (D.C. Calif. 1970).
30. *In re Harrell,* 2 Cal. 3d 675, 470 P.2d 640, 87 Cal. Rptr. 504 (1970).
31. *Younger v. Gilmore,* 404 U.S. 15 (1971), aff'g 319 F. Supp. 105 (N.D. Cal. 1970).

IV

Religious and Racial Discrimination

Under the First Amendment all persons are guaranteed the right to the free exercise of their religious beliefs. Recognizing that this right is "preferred," that is, of particular significance under the Constitution, the courts have held that freedom of religion does not terminate at the prison door.

Are there any restrictions on the free exercise of religion by prisoners?

Yes. Restrictions exist even on the more widely practiced religions. In the most recent cases, the courts have required prison administrators to show a compelling and substantial justification for any restrictions on the practice and exercise of religion in the prisons. Where security, safety, or prison discipline may be disrupted by religious exercises, the courts have upheld limitations. But these isolated examples indicate that on the whole, members of orthodox

61

religions are relatively free to exercise their religious beliefs, since the practice of such beliefs is not considered
to constitute a threat to prison authority.

Most prisons allow possession of the Bible, visits by, and
written communication with, ministers of the particular
faiths, the receipt of religious materials, the holding of
religious services, and the right to wear religious medals
and medallions. Indeed, traditional Christian worship is
encouraged in the belief that it will reinforce conservative
teachings with regard to sin, repentance and redemption.
It is, therefore, not surprising that there have been few
cases where law suits have been brought by other than
Muslim prisoners. In one, the court ordered a federal
institution to allow an inmate, who believed that he was
Christ incarnate, to write to the Pope, since prison officials
had failed to demonstrate that prison discipline or administration would be endangered by this correspondence.[1]
In another, a federal court ruled that the use of a shower
stall for Catholic communion impeded the free exercise
of religion for death-row inmates, and suggested that
prison officials accept a priest's offer to conduct mid-week
services in a more suitable setting.[2]

Do Muslim prisoners receive the same protection as prisoners of other religions?

Nearly all of the litigation over the right to the free
exercise of religion has involved suits by Muslims. For
the most part the Muslims have requested the courts to
grant them the same rights the prisons had already afforded
to members of other religious denominations. They have
asked, for example, for their own Bibles, religious reading
material, religious services and religiously acceptable diets
—rights fairly well established for prisoners of other

orthodox religions. In the First Amendment area, Muslims have also been instrumental in establishing new rights for prisoners of all religions. The reason that any discussion of the right to worship in prison inevitably revolves around the Muslims is that both the content and practice of their religion have been perceived as a threat to the administration of the penal institution. Muslims develop close unity among themselves; prison officials have a morbid fear of any organized group of inmates. Muslims, the majority of whom are black, do not refrain from raising the issue of racism while prison officials usually deny its very existence, much less its pervasiveness in prisons. Muslims are alienated from traditional prison procedures and practices (ranging from "rehabilitation" to diet); prison officials tend to view any prisoner or group that deviates from the prevailing model of corrections as a danger to the continuation of the closed prison society. As a result, prison administrators have attempted to prevent Muslims from exercising their religion in the prisons, primarily through regulations and disciplinary punishment.

Given this background, the courts are faced with three basic issues in suits initiated by Muslims. The first is whether the various substantive rights requested, that is, the right to possession of the Koran and the right to religious services in prison, are guaranteed by the First Amendment. The second is whether a prison discriminates against a particular variety of religious beliefs by permitting prisoners of some religions certain rights denied to Muslims. Finally, and of critical importance, the courts are called upon to rule on prison officials' claims that the various aspects of the practice of the Muslim religion in prison establishes a danger of some substantial interference with the orderly functioning and discipline of the institution.

Have courts supported the rights of Muslims to practice their religion?

Yes. On some issues, the courts have been consistent in supporting the rights of Muslim prisoners. It is now established, for example, that the Muslim sect is a religion under the First Amendment, thereby guaranteeing to Muslim prisoners the same rights as other inmates to practice and exercise their religious beliefs.[3] The recognition of the Muslim faith is important as well for non-orthodox religions, members of which may sue to exercise their rights in prison. As one court has declared, even in prison a person has an absolute right to embrace the religious beliefs of his choice and it is not the function of the court "to consider the merits or fallacies of a religion or to praise or condemn it, however excellent or fanatical or preposterous it may be."[4]

Similarly, the courts have had little difficulty in ordering that Muslims have an absolute right to receive, possess, and read the Holy Qur-An, the Muslim bible. The right to possess the bible has been granted either on the ground that the bibles of the major religious denominations are freely possessed by other prisoners or for the more basic reason that the constitutional guarantee to the free exercise of religion includes the right to read and study the religion's most important scriptures.[5]

Has the right of Muslims to practice their religion been restricted?

Yes. It is where Muslims have sought to extend their right to receive and read other Muslim literature that they have run into conflict with prison regulations and, in some cases, unsympathetic courts. A major dispute has centered around the desire of Muslims to receive their newspaper, *Muhammed Speaks*, and to receive Elijah Muhammed's book, *Message to the Black Man in America*.

On this question, the courts are split. Several have sustained prison officials' arguments that the newspaper and book are inflammatory and racist and, therefore, a threat to prison order and discipline.[6] Several others have ruled that Muslims have a right to receive these articles subject to censorship of offensive sections of the paper.[7] Most federal courts, however, now accept the clear-and-present danger test. As one court has stated:

> To justify the prohibition of religious literature, the prison officials must prove that the literature creates a clear and present danger of a breach of prison security or discipline or some other substantial interference with the orderly functioning of the institution.[8]

Muslims have also challenged prison regulations forbidding or restricting their religious services in prison. Most penal institutions provide for religious services for the major religious denominations. These services, usually held once a week, are performed by a minister who is allowed access to the prison both for the services and for individual counseling and prayer. Most courts have recognized that the refusal to allow Muslims the right to religious services and religious counseling in the prisons, while permitting it for other groups, is an impermissible discrimination against religious belief. Accordingly, these courts have granted Muslims the right to collective worship and visitation by Muslim ministers.[9]

Prisons and the courts have been less solicitous of requests by Muslims that they be permitted to correspond freely with Muslim ministers, and in particular, their spiritual leader, Elijah Muhammed. Most courts have deferred to prison regulations on mail communications and have only allowed these communications where other religious faiths in the prison are accorded similar rights, although one court, the Fifth Circuit, has held that there is a constitutional right to correspond with Elijah Muhammed.[10] Even that court, however, upheld censorship of these communications as a reasonable limitation on the free exercise of religion.

Must prison administrators make special provisions for the dietary and other needs of Muslim and orthodox prisoners?

They must make reasonable provisions. Muslims have strongly pressed their right to a pork-free diet as an integral part of their religious beliefs and practices. Few prisons honor these requests. Some courts have found that there is sufficient pork-free food in the prison's diet to sustain Muslims, and have for that reason denied requests for special food.

In one case, several members of the Muslim faith alleged that their rights under the first amendment had been denied because prison administrators had refused to provide them with a special diet and special feeding hours as required by their religion. During the month of December (Ramadan), the Muslims require diets without pork and with Akbar coffee and certain special pastries. In addition, this food must be eaten after sunset. The prison officials provided Jewish inmates one special meal a year at the time of Passover. The court discounted this aspect of the argument on the ground that the Muslims were asking for special privileges for a period of thirty days. The court held that the added cost of the food, the expense of preparation, and the additional security supervisors who would be required to move the Muslims during the night hours outweighed "whatever constitutional deprivation petitioners may claim."[11]

In another case involving the dietary requirements of Muslims, a slightly different decision was reached. Prisoners in the District of Columbia jail brought a suit against the jail administrators because a request for a minimum of one full-course, pork-free meal per day had been denied. The petition went on to plead release from confinement in the absence of compliance inasmuch as the resulting deprivation amounted to cruel and unusual punishment. According to the court the basic issue was "the degree to which officials of the District of Columbia jail are constitutionally compelled to accommodate the dietary laws of the Muslim faith."[12] The court concluded that there was no reason why the use of pork as seasoning could not be reduced, why "non-pork substitutes for main dishes of pork" could not be provided, why menus showing pork content could not be posted in advance, and why pork dishes could not be more evenly dispersed throughout the meal cycle. The court stated:

> That penal as well as judicial authorities respond to constitutional duties is vastly important to society as well as the prisoner. Treatment that degrades the inmate, invades his privacy, and frustrates the ability to choose pursuits through which he can manifest himself and gain self-respect erodes the very foundations upon which he can prepare for a socially useful

life. Religion in prison subserves the rehabilitative
function by providing an area within which the inmate
may reclaim his dignity and reassert his individuality.
But, quite ironically, while government provides prisoners with chapels, ministers, free sacred texts and
symbols, there subsists a danger that prison personnel
will demand from inmates the same obeisance in the
religious sphere that more rightfully they may require
in other aspects of prison life. This danger is not
chimerical. In recent years, against the directives of
the District of Columbia Commissioners, Muslim inmates in the custody of the Department of Corrections
have been deprived of the most basic religious liberties, which only by court order have been restored.[13]

May prisoners wear religious symbols?

Yes, and again the issue has been brought up by Muslim
prisoners. In one significant case it was shown that the
District of Columbia Department of Corrections purchased,
with public funds, religious medals for Catholic, Protestant,
and Jewish inmates. The prisoners were allowed to keep
these medals on their person and to wear them. No such
medals were purchased for the Muslims nor could they
be purchased anywhere within the prison. While attending
instructions in Islamic Culture, an inmate was given a
Muslim religious medal. He wore the medal openly until
it, along with all other Muslim medals in the prison, was
confiscated. There was no indication that the medals of
any other religion were confiscated. The court held that
the confiscation of the medals was a violation of the
prisoner's right not to be discriminated against because of
his religion, and that the prison administration must also

provide Muslim medals from public funds as long as other medals were so provided.[14]

Is racial segregation permitted in prison?

No. Following decisions by the United States Supreme Court invalidating various forms and practices of racial discrimination, the courts have been consistent in condemning racial segregation and discrimination in prisons.[15] They have rejected the arguments of prison officials that integration would lead to racial conflict and the breakdown of order (although in special situations where violence is imminent they have allowed temporary separation of the races), and have allowed blacks equal rights to reading material and religious exercises.

Despite these court decisions, racial discrimination continues to be as commonplace in our prisons as it is in the society at large. The general legal principles prohibiting discrimination have little relevance in the everyday administration of the prisons. Many penal institutions containing a large percentage of minority-group inmates are located in white rural communities, and in these prisons black inmates are subject to the directives and commands of the white guards recruited from these communities. Racism is a constant and substantial factor in these relationships, but most discriminatory practices are of such a nature as to pass under the rubric of discretionary acts of prison officials. It is most difficult to prove that any particular act was racially inspired since most prison officials are sophisticated enough to hide their real motivations. In one case, however, a federal district court awarded over $1400 to a black prisoner upon finding that he had been demoted in his job assignment—with a severe reduction in pay—because of his race.[16]

What can a prisoner do about racial discrimination?

Thus far no successful attack has been made on prison hiring policies, although a number of prison systems, recognizing the explosive potential of the volatile mixture of white guards and black inmates, have made some attempts to hire more blacks and to give greater training to white officers.

The counseling point for prisoners is simply that where racial considerations or discrimination can be proven as being the basis for a particular policy, decision, or act by prison officials, the courts will remedy the situation. The major problem inheres in the difficulty of proof; everyone knows that racism is rampant but few will acknowledge its presence in a particular situation.

NOTES

1. *Peck v. Ciccone*, 288 F.Supp. 329 (W.D. Mo. 1968).
2. *Glenn v. Wilkinson*, 309 F.Supp. 411 (W.D. Mo. 1970).
3. *Sewell v. Pegelow*, 291 F.2d 196 (4th Cir. 1961); *Fulwood v. Clemmer*, 206 F.Supp. 370 (D.D.C. 1961); *Sostre v. McGinnis*, 334 F.2d 906 (2d Cir. 1964).
4. *Fulwood v. Clemmer, supra* at 373.
5. *Walker v. Blackwell*, 411 F.2d 23 (5th Cir. 1969); *Long v. Parker*, 390 F.2d 816 (3d Cir. 1968).
6. *Knuckles v. Prasse*, 302 F.Supp. 1036 (E.D.Pa. 1969); *Abernathy v. Cunningham*, 393 F.2d 775 (4th Cir. 1968).
7. *Brown v. Peyton*, 437 F.2d 1228 (4th Cir. 1971); *Walker*

v. Blackwell, supra; Northern v. Nelson, 315 F.Supp. 687 (N.D. Calif. 1970).

8. *Long v. Parker, supra* at 822.
9. See, *e.g., Walker v. Blackwell, supra; Long v. Parker, supra; Cooper v. Pate,* 382 F.2d 518 (7th Cir. 1967).
10. *Walker v. Blackwell, supra.*
11. *Id.*
12. *Barnett v. Rogers,* 410 F.2d 995 (D.C. Cir. 1969).
13. *Id.* at 1002-1003.
14. *Fulwood v. Clemmer, supra.*
15. *Montgomery v. Oakley Training School,* 426 F.2d 269 (5th Cir. 1970); *Washington v. Lee,* 263 F.Supp. 327 (M.D. Ala. 1966).
16. *United States ex rel. Motley v. Rundle,* 340 F.Supp. 807 (E.D. Pa. 1972).

V

Political Rights

The essential political rights secured by the First Amendment—speech, association, assembly, and belief—have been given precious little breathing space in prison. The very nature of imprisonment has traditionally been held to require severe limitations on the right to assemble and associate with others. Moreover, speech has been restricted whenever prison officials claim that it endangers prison security or discipline. And beliefs, though not as susceptible to manipulation or destruction by prison authorities, nevertheless have been effectively controlled by various forms of punishment—segregation, harassment, denial of parole, and so forth—which are often imposed on the prisoner who makes known his unpopular political beliefs.

Do prisoners have any political rights?
The regulation and restriction of political activities are not matters that are usually covered by written rules. Each particular assertion by a prisoner of his political right has been dealt with on an ad hoc basis, with individual decisions

varying greatly not only from prison to prison, but from
inmate to inmate within a single institution. Therefore, it
is impossible to advise prisoners of their political rights,
at least in terms of what kinds of speech and other political
activity may be tolerated at any given time in any prison.
We are just too far from a rule of law in this area to be
able to do that.

May prisoners be punished for expressing their political beliefs?

The law is unclear. Several courts have held that First
Amendment rights follow a person into prison and may
be restricted only where their exercise creates a clear and
present danger to the orderly administration of the institution. Unfortunately, however, the courts have generally
subordinated first amendment rights to the prison's determination that the speech or political activity threatened
prison discipline or security. Despite occasional flourishes
of constitutional rhetoric stressing the importance of First
Amendment rights for prisoners, the "hands-off" policy
still has a secure grip in this area.

With the changing nature of our prison population,
claims to political rights will in all probability be intensified
in the future. While some may quarrel over the number
of political prisoners in our institutions, there can be no
doubt that blacks, Chicanos, draft resisters, and other political dissidents, as well as inmates who are politicized as
a result of their exposure to our correctional system, will
continue to push for the right to free political expression
in prison.

The Second Circuit Court of Appeals' decision in the

Sostre[2] case included a discussion of the right to political expression and beliefs. Sostre had been punished by prison authorities for expressing "radical beliefs" in a letter to his sister and for collecting the writings of black nationalists and revolutionaries. In addition, he was punished for refusing to answer a warden's questions about the Republic of New Africa. The Court of Appeals ruled that this punishment was illegal since it "would permit prison authorities to manipulate and crush thoughts under the guise of regulation."[3] Other courts have also ruled that a prisoner's *beliefs* are protected under the Constitution, but have placed strict limits on the expression of these beliefs.

Do prisoners have a right to form political organizations?

This issue has only recently been raised.

The relative powerlessness of prisoners has led some to attempt to organize prisoner unions and political organizations. In California, a group called the United Prisoners' Union has drawn up a bill of rights for prisoners and is attempting to gain access to the prison populations with the hope, ultimately, of organizing the prisoners into the union. A leader in this movement has stated:

> Until we unionize we are doomed eternally to the cruel cycle of poverty, prison, and parole and more poverty. In the widening class struggle we are the lowest of the low, denied the most basic constitutional rights and powerless to deal with an incredible oppression.

In Pennsylvania, a loosely knit organization known as the Imprisoned Citizens' Union has initiated a wide-ranging lawsuit in federal court challenging virtually every facet of prison life in the state's prisons.

In the Washington State Penitentiary at Walla Walla, an inmate government, known as the Resident Governmental Council, has been initiated with the approval of state officials. At the core of the experiment, which involves extensive reforms and liberalization of prison rules, is a representative council of prisoners, elected by prisoners, and a written constitution. The purpose of this change in prison social structure is to enable prisoners to have a say in the determination of prison regulations and policies, in the disciplinary processes, and in their daily life patterns.

Perhaps the most significant attempt at prisoner organization has been the Prisoners' Labor Union at Green Haven Prison. The organizing effort among the prisoners at Green Haven, a maximum-security facility fifty miles from New York City, began in the summer of 1971. Despite initial harassment and punishment by the administration, the movement continued to grow. With the impetus of the Attica Prison rebellion of September 1971, and the assistance of lawyers from the Prisoners' Rights Project of the Legal Aid Society of New York City, which is counsel to the union, the movement finally coalesced. A constitution was drafted and adopted in the late fall of 1971, and authorization cards were circulated among and signed by the vast majority of the population. Simultaneously, a Public Advisory Committee, comprised of labor leaders, liberal politicians, and public figures, was created to support the Union. Most significantly, the Prisoners' Labor Union also gained the support and assistance of a strong, progressive labor union, District 65, Distributive Workers of America, whose executive committee authorized affiliation with the Prisoners' Labor Union, provided both membership ratified it.

In February, 1972, the Union, with a membership of thirteen hundred out of a population of eighteen hundred, publicly announced its formation and demanded recognition by the New York Department of Correctional Services. The demand was rejected. The union then filed a petition for certification as collective bargaining agent for all the prisoners at Green Haven before the New York Public Employment Relations Board. Since prisoners work for the state and are paid by it, the Green Haven organization is considered a public employees' union, and as such is prohibited under New York State law from striking.

As of this writing, the petition for certification is pending before the board in Albany, New York, and the movement is spreading to the other prisons in the state. It is the belief of the Prisoners' Labor Union at Green Haven, its lawyers and many of its supporters, that the Union concept is an idea whose time has come, an idea which will take seed and blossom in prisons around the country as perhaps the best way for prisoners to have some real measure of control over their own lives.

Should prison officers be permitted to regulate inmate political activities?

No. It should be stressed, however, that these changes, as with most experiments of this nature, have caused resentment among correctional officials who fear that prison discipline and security are jeopardized by liberal reforms. The shift away from a strict security function has placed the correctional officers in a position to which they are not accustomed. This conflict will probably appear wherever reforms in prison life lead to a significant decrease in the discretion and power of prison guards.

The indications are clear that, with few exceptions, prison authorities will not tolerate political organizing and litigation will be required to test the right of prisoners to organize and attempt to present their collective demands for a change in prison practices.

Prison officials must not have unlimited discretion to permit or prohibit political activities. At the very least, these organizations should be protected unless prison authorities demonstrate that their existence or activities create a clear and present danger of subversion of legitimate prison administration. Officials should be required to adopt rules and regulations covering what activity will be subject to punishment; these rules must in turn be limited to prohibit only those activities which in fact pose a clear and present danger to prison security and discipline. Peaceful organizing, petitioning, meetings, advocacy and assembly should be protected. Disagreement with political thought or speech cannot be valid grounds for a finding of clear and present danger; speech is always disruptive in that sense. Assembly in private by prisoners should only be prohibited on *evidence,* not mere speculation, of unlawful activity. And formation of organizations of inmates for the purpose of presenting unified demands or suggestions concerning prison life is essential to the prisoners' right to have some say in their day-to-day existence.

NOTES

1. *Sostre v. McGinnis,* 442 F.2d 178 (2nd Cir. 1971).
2. *Id.* at 202.
3. *Id.*

VI

Privacy and Personal Appearance

Prisoners have shown increasing interest in changing prison policy which currently restricts their rights to freedom of dress, personal appearance, and privacy.

The right to privacy ceases to exist upon entry into the penal institution. Prisoners' mail is censored, and in many prisons their visits with family, friends, and even attorneys are monitored by prison officials.

Do prison authorities have the right to search inmates?
Yes, with only occasional minor restrictions and safeguards. In spite of the fact that in recent years some prisons have relaxed their policies, making correspondence a good deal freer and visits confidential, particularly those with attorneys, prison officials continue to insist on the power to search prisoners and their effects at any time and for any reasons. They say they need this power in order to prevent smuggling, possession of contraband, and the fashioning

of weapons or tools within the prison which could be used for assault or escape purposes. Legally, of course, the usual constitutional processes under the Fourth Amendment, including the requirements of a search warrant and probable cause prior to searches and seizures, do not apply in prison. This should not mean, however, that prison officials should be free to conduct searches for whatever reason, at whatever time, and in whatever manner they please. Arbitrariness and capriciousness have no more of a place in an official's decision to search than in a decision concerning the prisoner's free exercise of religion. To be sure, substantial limitations on one's privacy can be expected in prison, but this is not inconsistent with reasonable rules and procedures, made known in advance to the inmates.

In one case where this issue has arisen, a Maryland Court has issued regulations governing searches of inmates at Patuxent Institution. The searches must be conducted with "maximum respect and minimal discomfort" to the inmates, only items prohibited by the conduct rules may be confiscated, and all items removed in searches of cells must be replaced without damage. Further, the court stated that inmates have a right to be present during a search of their cells and must be given a written list of all items confiscated.[1]

Do prisoners have the right to control their personal appearance?

Traditionally, no. The familiar scene of prisoners dressed identically in gray garb, short haircuts, with no mustaches or beards has changed little over the years. The regulations requiring such appearance exist in virtually all prisons, with few exceptions. Often supported by prison officials as necessary health and safety measures, in reality they deprive the inmate of his sense of identity and presence and enforce regimentation in the prison. Erving Goffman, in his *Essays on Asylums,* describes the "mortification" which prisoners are forced to undergo. One aspect of this process is the personal defacement of inmates by the prison:

> On admission to a total institution . . . the individual is likely to be stripped of his usual appearance and of the equipment and services by which he maintains it, thus suffering a personal defacement. Clothing, combs, needle and thread, cosmetics, towels, soap, shaving sets, bathing facilities—all these may be taken away or denied him, although some may be kept in inaccessible storage, to be returned if and when he leaves.[2]

Have any changes taken place?

Little progress has been made in attempts to change this process. At least two states, Pennsylvania and California, now allow prisoners to wear clothes other than institutionally issued material.

Other aspects of personal appearance are also subject to suppression at the say-so of prison officials. Jewelry, artifacts, and other personal items are allowed only by permission. In a case involving Erika Huggins, a federal court in Connecticut ruled that where a prison regulation limited the jewelry women prisoners might wear to a wristwatch, earrings, a ring and necklace with a religious medal on it, no infringement of any constitutional rights existed.[3] Both prison administrators and the courts must be pushed on this issue and be made to recognize that dehumanization by forced conformity is a dangerous reality in our prisons.

With respect to physical appearance, some progress has been made. The issue most frequently raised concerns the right of male prisoners to have long hair, beards, and mustaches. In one case, Bobby Seale, while awaiting trial in Connecticut, sued to vindicate his right to retain his beard. Prison officials sought to justify the prohibition against beards by citing them as a potential health hazard in the spread of lice among prisoners, but the court found there to be no problem of lice at the jail and ruled that Seale could wear his short beard and goatee.[4]

Most courts, however, have denied requests that prisoners be allowed to determine the length of their hair or wear beards or mustaches. They have stated that prison regulations in this regard are neither arbitrary nor harsh, and are supported by reasons of health (presumably long hair leads to health problems for men but not women) and the need to be able to identify prisoners. Some courts have in fact suggested that all men look alike in long hair and beards.

May any constitutional grounds be invoked to attack regulations concerning personal appearance?

Yes. First, unless prison officials can advance a reason for women prisoners, but not men, to wear long hair, there would seem to be a plain violation of the man's right to equal protection of the laws since arbitrary discrimination based on sex is unconstitutional. Generally, the reasons given for requiring short hair are prison sanitation, discipline, and morale. Assuming a basis for any of these, the question of why men and not women is still not answered. Therefore, the equal protection argument seems compelling.

Of course, since prisons are segregated on the basis of sex and different prison officials are responsible for separate penal institutions within one prison system, it will not always be possible to raise the equal protection issue. This leaves the argument that the personal appearance of a person is his right to determine, even in prison, unless the officials can support a contrary regulation by compelling reasons. If the burden is placed on prison officials, they will be required to do more than mouth the usual incantations of sanitariness and discipline. They will have to show how these concerns are affected by long hair and facial hair. However, if the courts adhere to the theory that a prisoner loses his rights as he enters prison and the prison official's mere assertion of a need for a particular regulation is sufficient to uphold that rule, obviously the regulations will be sustained.

The whole process of cutting inmates' hair really amounts to a grisly flashback into an age when it was a recognized, acceptable practice of our penal institutions to disfigure the prisoner in some fashion so as to mark him, at least for some period of time, to be held up to scorn by the public at large. This was an attempt not only to deter others, but to break down the offender to an acceptable level of subserviency. During the early development of our legal system the cutting off of ears, fingers, or other appendages of the inmate was sanctioned. Even after the sentence had been completed, society would know that this particular individual had been condemned. Our legal system, in its more dreary past, also sanctioned the cutting of hair as one method of placing the prison mark on the inmate. This was particularly true of women convicted of

prostitution who were turned out into the street bald, so
that all would know they had been punished under the law.

NOTES

1. *McCray v. Maryland,* 10 Cr.L.Rptr. 2132 (Cir.Ct. Md.
   Nov. 11, 1971).
2. Goffman, *Essays on Asylums,* p. 20 (Anchor Books,
   1961).
3. *Seale v. Manson,* 326 F.Supp. 1375 (D. Conn. 1971).
4. *Id.*

VII

Medical Care, Rehabilitation, and Physical Security of Prisoners

Lack of adequate medical, dental, and psychiatric care is the rule in all penal institutions. The primary cause of this situation is the lack of competent medical personnel to treat the thousands of men and women who pass through the correctional system each year. In many prisons, only the most serious ailments are treated and often these are the subject of haphazard and mediocre care; minor ailments are often ignored for lack of a doctor or nurse or for more callous reasons—such as the refusal by a guard to allow a prisoner to attend sick call.

Do prisoners have a right to be provided with medical treatment?

Yes. An increasing number of suits have challenged the quality and nature of medical treatment afforded prisoners. The early attitude of the courts—a manifestation of the "hands-off" policy—was to dismiss all suits which raised questions concerning prison medical practices. Prison officials were deemed the best judges of what treatment was required, and the courts stated that they were not equipped to question these decisions.

That rigid attitude has been relaxed only slightly over the past decade; the general rule today is that proof of wilful denial of medical care resulting in physical pain or injury establishes a violation of an inmate's constitutional rights. One court, in adopting a standard similar to that often expressed in the cruel and unusual punishment context, has ruled that the conduct must amount to a "barbarous act" that "shocks the conscience" in order to entitle the prisoner to judicial relief.[1]

Who decides what treatment a prisoner is entitled to receive?

Prison officials, in practice. The courts have provided very little in the way of concrete relief to prisoners because most cases have involved disputes between prisoners and medical officials as to whether medical treatment was sufficient. The courts are most likely to believe the testimony of the doctors and other prison officials that the treatment was adequate. In addition, the courts have uniformly held that neither negligence nor a mere difference of opinion between the prisoner and prison officials will support an allegation of inadequate medical care under the federal civil rights act.

While the prisoner is not, according to the courts, the ultimate judge of what medical treatment is necessary or proper, where he can demonstrate obvious neglect or intentional mistreatment, a remedy will be afforded. Similarly, prison officials may not overrule a doctor's medical prescription concerning a prisoner's treatment.

Under these guidelines courts have found that constitutional rights of prisoners were denied in a variety of situations; these include the refusal of prison medical officials to treat an inmate's heart ailment, the refusal to give an operation recommended by the prison doctor, the denial of access to medical treatment for a prisoner with a broken neck, and the withholding of medical attention to a prisoner suffering from bullet wounds which resulted in the amputation of one of the prisoner's limbs.[2]

What remedy exists for prisoners who receive negligent or inadequate medical treatment?

Several rather ineffective remedies exist for the prisoner where the failure to provide adequate medical care does not rise to constitutional dimensions. Federal prisoners may sue under the Tort Claims Act for money damages for negligent treatment or non-treatment of medical problems, even though such suits may interfere with prison discipline.[3] Similarly, many states have statutes enabling prisoners to sue for medical malpractice or negligence and state courts have awarded damages to prisoners in cases where their claims would not have been recognized by federal courts. New York State courts have afforded recovery to a prisoner who suffered great pain because of the prison's failure to administer drugs to him and to an inmate of a state hospital who was committed on the basis of a negligently prepared diagnosis of his mental condition by a state doctor.

Do narcotic addicts have a right to treatment in prison?

Several suits have been initiated on behalf of narcotic addicts who suffer withdrawal symptoms asking the courts to order methadone detoxification programs. The theory of these cases is that narcotic-substitution therapy is the principal medically indicated course of treatment for drug withdrawal and, therefore, prison officials are under a duty to institute this method of treatment for inmates. Courts have held that when current medical practice indicates a particular course of treatment, denial of such treatment constitutes cruel and unusual punishment. Courts may soon hold that forcing prisoners to undergo unalleviated drug withdrawal constitutes cruel and unusual punishment as a denial of needed medical treatment.

Methadone detoxification is in increasing use in various prisons. New York City prisons have been using methadone detoxification as a standard practice for over a year; the Maryland legislature recently adopted a measure allowing its use in all state and county jails; and in Philadelphia, in response to a lawsuit, prison officials have instituted a methadone detoxification program in its detention facilities.

Do prisoners have a right to education and training?

No. One of the central vices of prison life is the enforced idleness that inmates must endure. Few prisons provide any meaningful rehabilitation opportunities; in most prisons psychiatric and psychological counseling are non-existent; and vocational training is plainly outdated and inadequate.

The gap between the rhetoric of corrections—rehabilitation, education, training, treatment—and the reality of prison life—idleness, despair, solitude, dehumanization— grows greater each year. The *Manual of Correctional Standards* of the American Correctional Association states that the prison's "basic purpose" is "the rehabilitation of those sent there by society." This sentiment is echoed in state statutes, prison regulations, court decisions, legislative reports and other official pronouncements, but most prison officials continue to believe that "rehabilitation" is achieved only when the prisoner accepts without question the authoritarian structure and policies of the institution. It should be made clear that we speak of rehabilitation in terms of the opportunity for education and training and not in terms of thought control or institutional conformity.

Despite the rhetoric, no court has directly held that a prisoner is entitled to rehabilitation. Nevertheless, court decisions in clearly analogous areas have laid the groundwork for what may eventually become a successful attack on the lack of rehabilitation services and programs in our prisons. Cases, including those in the Supreme Court, involving commitments to mental hospitals, juvenile jails, and other institutions have suggested that officials have a constitutional obligation to provide adequate treatment and/or rehabilitation programs for the inmates of these institutions.[4]

These decisions have been based on the theory that the sole reason for the commitment in the first place was for treatment and that the lack of treatment removes the justification for incarceration. Of course, since prisons are meant to punish, prevent, and deter as well as rehabilitate, it is much more difficult to persuade the courts to apply this principle to the treatment of prisoners. But as rehabilitation becomes the primary purpose and rationale of incarceration, the logical extension of the "right to treatment" cases is to require, as a constitutional matter, meaningful rehabilitation programs. At a minimum, prisons should provide inmates, where needed, with up-to-date vocational and educational training, and psychological and medical treatment.

The right to rehabilitation was recognized in a decision concerning Patuxent Institution, Maryland's correctional facility for defective delinquents.[5] In a sweeping opinion that ordered extensive changes in virtually every aspect of institutional life, the court ruled that Patuxent inmates have a constitutional right to be treated for the mental condition that led to their crimes. This decision, if sustained on appeal, could be the link needed to firmly establish the right to rehabilitation for convicted felons.

In some cases, courts have indicated that the failure of a prison to provide rehabilitation opportunities may be considered in determining whether confinement in the institution amounts to cruel and unusual punishment. The leading case is *Holt v. Sarver*,[6] a class action that sought to upgrade Arkansas prison conditions, in which the court considered the constitutional necessity for rehabilitation in imprisonment of adult criminal offenders. In discussing the need for rehabilitative treatment, the court stated that it was not prepared to constitutionally require rehabilitative attempts as to convicts, but held:

> That however, is not quite the end of the matter. The absence of an affirmative program of training and rehabilitation may have constitutional significance where in the absence of such a program conditions and practices exist which militate against reform and rehabilitation.

The Court of Appeals for the Eighth Circuit made a similar point in prohibiting imposition of corporal punishment when it declared that "corporal punishment generates hate towards the keepers who punish and towards the system which permits it. . . . It frustrates correctional and rehabilitative goals."[7]

In the same vein, the Supreme Court of Pennsylvania has held that the lack of rehabilitative programs resulting in forced idleness was a factor that, considered with other substandard conditions, could constitute a system of cruel and unusual punishment.[8] It can be argued from these cases that while the prison may not be required to provide educational and vocational programs to its inmates, it should be forbidden to allow conditions that make rehabilitation difficult to achieve.

Do prisoners have a right to be protected against sexual assault?

In recent years, several degrading and unconstitutional facets of prison life have become exposed to public view and scrutiny. These problems have been highlighted again and again in court cases, administrative studies, and legislative investigations. Perhaps the most dramatic and sickening aspect of these disclosures, however, concerns the widespread and often uncontrolled pattern of assaults by prisoners and guards upon prisoners.

No penal institution in the country remains free of this problem. In Philadelphia, for example, the Davis Report on Sexual Assaults in the Philadelphia Prison System conservatively estimated that during a twenty-six-month period there were approximately two thousand sexual assaults involving approximately fifteen hundred individual victims and thirty-five hundred individual aggressors in Philadelphia prisons.

What remedies does a prisoner have if he is assaulted?

Presently, the three possible remedies for assault are criminal prosecution of offenders, punishment of offenders after internal prison disciplinary proceedings, and civil suit for damages.

Criminal prosecution

All concede the ineffectiveness of criminal prosecution as a deterrent to prison assaults. Prosecutions are made in only a minute percentage of actual prison assaults. In most cases the victim is too scared to complain, fearing both physical retribution and the inevitable ridicule and embarrassment of disclosure. Complaints are discouraged by guards, and prisoners are sometimes punished for merely complaining, for they will be confined to their cells, ostensibly for their own protection. Moreover, while a distinction has properly been made between forced sexual attacks and consensual relationships, this distinction overlooks the fact that forcible sexual assaults are sometimes a cause of "consensual" homosexuality.

Prison Disciplinary Procedures

A second response by the authorities to complaints of sexual attacks on prisoners has been the use of prison disciplinary procedures against the alleged offender. For obvious reasons, most internal disciplinary proceedings like criminal prosecutions, concern allegations of forced sexual attacks as opposed to consensual homosexual relationships.

There are more internal proceedings than criminal prosecutions—primarily because the procedures involved afford very little, if any, protection for the accused, and thereby facilitate action against the alleged offender. Since the burden of proof is so slight and the protections afforded the accused so minimal, these proceedings facilitate the prison administration's punishment of suspected offenders and thereby provides a tool for dealing with those who commit sexual assaults. Unfortunately, it seems clear that the lack of due process leads to mistakes in final determinations. Moreover, for the same reason that prisoners are reluctant to initiate criminal prosecutions against sexual offenders, they are equally reluctant to make any complaint to prison officials that may result in disciplinary hearings.

Civil Suit

A third possible remedy—a civil damage suit against the offender—provides even less hope of relief. All the factors noted above with respect to criminal prosecutions, of course, act as a deterrent to civil actions, and since the overwhelming majority of prisoners are indigent, the victim cannot secure counsel to bring suit and thus no relief is available.

Another possible legal approach for the victim is a civil suit against prison officials for failing to protect him from sexual attacks from other inmates. In federal prisons there is a remedy under the Federal Tort Claims Act, which provides that prison officials must exercise ordinary care for prisoners' protection and safety. If they fail to meet this standard, they are liable for damages when one inmate is physically or sexually assaulted by another. If the prison negligently classifies inmates or allows dangerous inmates to assault others, the victim has legal recourse under the statute. In a case involving a federal penitentiary in Georgia, the victim of a vicious physical assault by another inmate sued prison officials under the Federal Tort Claims Act. The court found that the prison officials were negligent in failing to prevent the assault because they failed to properly classify the assaulting prisoner (he was psychotic and had a history of physical assaults) and in failing to keep him from an area where the victim was working.[9]

In state prisons, similar relief is available under either the federal civil-rights act, or under applicable state tort law. An example of a successful legal action under both theories is provided by a Mississippi case, where the court sustained a damage action against the superintendent of the prison by a fourteen year old who, while confined in a county prison, was shot and blinded by an armed trustee. The court found the superintendent legally liable for the gross negligence of the trustee.[10]

A New Jersey court has gone even further, stating that a jailer has the duty to employ the care of a reasonable and prudent person in the protection of prisoners against *reasonably* foreseeable risks. The court ruled that a prisoner could sue prison officials for injuries received in an attack by another prisoner even though the officials had no direct notice of the attacker's plans.[11]

The applicability of these theories to the inmate who is sexually assaulted in the prison seems clear. Many sexual assaults that occur in prisons result from improper classifications, inadequate or negligent guard supervision, forced idleness of prisoners, and defects in the structural design of prisons. The failure to protect prisoners, particularly those who predictably will become victims of sexual attack, should properly be laid to prison officials who have done little to correct this situation. Until they feel the pinch of lawsuits, it is doubtful that the incidence of prison assaults will be appreciably reduced.

NOTES

1. *United States ex rel. Hyde v. McGinnis,* 429 F.2d 864 (2d Cir. 1970).
2. See, *e.g., Talley v. Stephens,* 247 F.Supp. 683 (E.D. Ark. 1965); *Sawyer v. Sigler,* 320 F.Supp. 690 (D.Neb. 1970); *Tobert v. Eyman,* 434 F.2d 625 (9th Cir. 1970); *Martinez v. Mancusi,* 443 F.2d 921 (2d Cir. 1970).
3. *United States v. Muniz,* 374 U.S. 150 (1963).
4. See, *e.g., In re Gault,* 387 U.S. 1 (1967); *Covington v. Harris,* 419 F.2d 617 (D.C. Cir. 1969); *Rouse v. Cameron,* 373 F.2d 451 (D.C. Cir. 1966) and *Wyatt v. Stickney,* 325 F.Supp. 781 (N.D. Ala. 1971).
5. *McCray v. Maryland,* 10 Cr. L. Rptr. 2132 (Cir. Ct. Md. Nov. 11, 1971).
6. 309 F.Supp. 362 (E.D. Ark. 1970), aff'd, 442 F.2d 304 (8th Cir. 1971).
7. *Jackson v. Bishop,* 404 F.2d 571 (8th Cir. 1968).

8. *Commonwealth ex rel. Bryant v. Hendrick,* 444 Pa. 83 (1971).
9. *Cohen v. United States,* 252 F.Supp. 679 (N.D. Ga. 1966).
10. *Roberts v. Williams,* 302 F.Supp. 972 (N.D. Miss. 1969).
11. *Harris v. State,* 118 N.J. Super. 384 (1972).

VIII

Jail Conditions—Pre-Trial Confinement

However desperate the conditions in many state prisons, they are far better than those that prevail in the thousands of jails around the country used to detain persons awaiting trial and to imprison convicts serving short prison sentences. The jails are an unmitigated disgrace. They are overcrowded, understaffed, unsanitary, and structurally deteriorating. They give little protection from physical and sexual assaults, provide virtually no programs, and spend almost their entire budgets on security. In short, they exist only to warehouse those persons charged with crime who are too poor to post bail for their release.

Detentioners have many of the same legal problems faced by the prisoners in state prisons discussed in other chapters. They too are subject to substandard physical conditions; they are denied First Amendment rights of communication; and they are disciplined and punished without even the rudimentary protections of due process of law. But jails deserve separate attention since the legal rights involved are substantially affected by the fact that jail inmates are

for the most part detentioners, not prisoners, and are, under
the law, presumed to be innocent. Theoretically, at least,
the detention is for the sole purpose of ensuring a defendant's appearance at trial, and is not for punishment. In
practice, prisoners are usually provided with better conditions and a detentioner can expect to have his physical
living conditions improve if he or she is convicted and
sentenced to a state prison.

Of immediate concern to detentioners are two problems—
the reduction of bail to a reasonable level and the proper
preparation of the case. Much has been written on these
topics, and repetition here would serve no purpose. Suffice
it to say that the money bail system as presently constituted
is the most irrational and oppressive aspect of our entire
system of criminal justice. It puts a price tag on liberty and
serves to preventively detain only the poor.

What are the major problems of detentioners?

Poor physical conditions and inadequate physical protection. A flurry of recent cases involving jail conditions
in various towns and cities has resulted in decisions de-
claring many of these conditions unconstitutional. In Pennsylvania, the State Supreme Court has recently sustained
a lower court's ruling that the conditions at Holmesburg
County Prison in Philadelphia were cruel and unusual.[1]
The facts in this case reflect conditions that exist in most
jails, and provide a basis upon which suits may be brought
to alleviate the incarceration of detentioners. The court
found that the cells were overcrowded, infested with
vermin, and became soaked after heavy rain. The bedding
was dirty and inadequate personal items were provided.
Medical and social services were inadequate, the kitchen

facilities dirty, and virtually no educational or vocational programs were available to detainees. Even more seriously, the lack of an adequate number of trained guards allowed sexual attacks to take place, and the guards themselves were found to have directly participated in physical attacks and beatings of inmates.

Under these circumstances, the court held that confinement of detentioners constituted cruel and unusual punishment, not only for those who were the actual subjects of the attacks and who medically suffered from the substandard conditions, but for all detentioners since they were all subject to the dangerous conditions. In this approach the Pennsylvania court adopted the theory, first articulated by the federal court in Arkansas,[2] that the totality of substandard conditions in prisons can amount to cruel and unusual punishment for the convicts incarcerated in them.

Similar cases have resulted in strong opinions condemning pre-trial jail facilities in Detroit, Michigan; Chicago, Illinois; New Orleans, Louisiana; Toledo, Ohio; Gallup, New Mexico; and Alameda County, California.[3] In these cases, the courts have held that the physical conditions in the jails were so intolerable as to require judicial intervention. In reaching these conclusions, the courts have not relied solely on the Eighth Amendment principle governing the concept of cruel and unusual punishment; they have, in addition, recognized that pre-trial detainees are entitled to more rights than convicted prisoners. And following the Arkansas federal court, these courts too have adopted the theory that all the conditions in a particular institution must be examined to determine their impact on an inmate's rights. Thus, the courts will be prone to intercede where prisoners can show a combination of any of the following: substandard and overcrowded living conditions, inadequate protection against attacks either by guards or other prisoners, and lack of programs and inadequate medical and social services.

Do detentioners have more rights than sentenced prisoners?

Yes. In finding conditions in a local jail to be unconstitutional, Ohio Federal Court Judge Young stated:

> It is hard to think of any reason why the conditions of confinement should be permitted for those who are only in jail awaiting trial, and are, according to our law, presumed to be innocent of any wrongdoing. For centuries, under our law, punishment before conviction has been forbidden. The Constitution does not authorize the treatment of a pre-trial detainee as a convict. . . .
>
> Obviously no person may be punished except by due process of law. Here the evidence shows that at best, those who are in the Lucas County Jail pending trial of charges against them suffer the same treatment as those who are confined there for punishment.[4]

The Fifth Circuit Court of Appeals has articulated the differing bases of imprisonment of convicted and unconvicted persons:

> Incarceration after conviction is imposed to punish, to deter, and to rehabilitate the convict. . . . Some freedom to accomplish these ends must of necessity be afforded prison personnel. Conversely, where incarceration is imposed prior to conviction, deterrence,

punishment, and retribution are not legitimate functions of the incarcerating officials. Their role is but a temporary holding operation and their necessary freedom of action is concomitantly diminished.

Plaintiffs here were unconvicted misdemeanants held for bond. The purpose of incarceration of them was simply detention in order to assure presence at trial. Punitive measures in such a context are out of harmony with the presumption of innocence.[5]

When one considers the rights to free communications, visitation, reading material, and proper medical care under these standards, it seems clear that restrictions which may arguably be legitimate in prisons cannot be justified for detainees. Some courts have made this important distinction. A New York federal court has ruled that jail officials were not justified in placing Angela Davis in isolation in the Women's House of Detention. The court held that she was a pre-trial detainee, presumed to be innocent, and isolation was unnecessary to ensure her appearance at trial.[6] Thus, incarceration in isolation was in violation of her right to equal protection of the law. The court reasoned that only those conditions necessary to the security aspect of short-term detention could be imposed on those who, because of poverty, could not afford bail. Another federal court has held that restrictions on beards and goatees, while possibly valid for convicted prisoners, could not be applied to pre-trial detainees.[7] Prison officials should be made to justify on grounds of security *all* regulations which restrict rights of detentioners. If they fail to show that the particular rule is necessary and reasonably related to security, it should be declared unconsitutional since no other legal theory can support any limitation on the rights of detainees.

Furthermore, it seems plausible to argue that, at a minimum, the services, facilities, and opportunities offered to detentioners be adequate according to prevailing community standards. Inadequacy amounts to punishment; if the presumption of innocence is to be meaningful for detentioners, it should find expression in judicial protection of their right to emerge, both physically and mentally, in no worse condition than they were at the time of their detention.

If the standard of "adequacy" were adopted, it is highly unlikely that any jail in the country could avoid making substantial improvements in its physical conditions, services, and treatment of detentioners.

Are detentioners entitled to vote?

Detentioners and convicted prisoners alike often ask whether they are entitled to vote while in jail. The answer for convicts at this time is very clearly no. And while a 1969 Supreme Court decision seemed to indicate that detentioners likewise could be denied this right,[8] the Court has agreed to hear argument on another case raising this question and a more clear-cut answer may be forthcoming.[9] Certainly, there is virtually no justification for denying detentioners the right to vote since they are in jail only for lack of money and have been convicted of no crime.

NOTES

1. *Commonwealth ex rel. Bryant v. Hendrick*, 444 Pa. 83 (1971). Another suit challenging Philadelphia's prisons resulted in a 264 page opinion holding the entire prison system unconstitutional and ordering large scale reforms.

Jackson v. Hendrick, No. 71-2437 (Phila. Ct. Com. Pleas, April 7, 1972) (en banc).

2. *Holt v. Sarver,* 309 F.Supp. 362 (E.D. Ark. 1970); aff'd, 442 F.2d 304 (8th Cir. 1971).

3. *Jones v. Wittenberg,* 323 F.Supp. 93 (N.D. Ohio, 1971); *Hamilton v. Love,* 328 F.Supp. 1182 (E.D. Ark., 1971); *Morris v. Travisono,* 310 F.Supp. 857 (D.R.I. 1970); *Wayne County Jail Inmates v. Wayne County Board of Commissioners* (Circuit Court, Wayne County, Mich. 1971 No. 173217); *Brenneman v. Madigan,* 343 F.Supp. 128 (N.D. Cal. 1972).

4. *Jones v. Wittenberg,* 323 F.Supp. 92 (N.D. Ohio, 1971).

5. *Anderson v. Nosser,* 438 F.2d 183, 190 (5th Cir. 1971).

6. *Davis v. Lindsay,* 321 F.Supp. 1134 (S.D.N.Y. 1970).

7. *Seale v. Manson,* 326 F.Supp. 1375 (D. Conn. 1971).

8. *McDonald v. Bd. of Election Commissioners,* 394 U.S. 802 (1969).

9. *Goosby v. Osser,* October Term, 1972, No. 71-6316.

IX

Parole

Parole has evolved as an alternative to continued imprisonment: prisoners are selected for release and, theoretically, are provided with controls, assistance, and guidance to help them serve the remainder of their sentence in the free community. Over sixty percent of all prisoners in our correctional institutions will be released on parole and the number increases yearly. Many others are eligible and are considered for release, but are denied parole and serve their full sentence. The parole-granting process is, therefore, the most critical concern for the vast majority of all prisoners since it constitutes, in effect, a resentencing.

When may a prisoner be released on parole?

Under most sentencing procedures, broad power is vested in the parole board to determine the length of an offender's term of imprisonment. Varying from jurisdiction to jurisdiction, a prisoner generally becomes eligible for parole when some part of his maximum term is served (one third or one half), or at the end of the minimum sentence. In some cases, the time may be reduced if the prisoner has earned good time or work-time credit and, under some statutes, a prisoner may be eligible for parole as soon as he begins his term of imprisonment.

What is the procedure for granting parole?

Upon application by a prisoner for parole, a hearing is held before an institutional staff board which compiles a case history of the applicant based both on records available to the board and on information provided by the prisoners. The prisoner then goes before the parole board which evaluates all the records and ultimately decides on the parole application.

The decision to grant or deny parole is made in most cases on the basis of such factors as an offender's prior history, his readiness for release, and his need for supervision and assistance in the community prior to the expiration of his sentence. Typically, however, the decision as to whether parole should be granted is made on insufficient and often biased information. The information gathered by institutional officials about the parole applicant is usually compiled from meager and possibly inaccurate prison records and is often fitted into a highly stereotyped format. Under current practices, the institutional report is usually the decisive factor in a parole board's determination.

For what reasons may parole be denied?

Apparently for any reason or no reason at all. Most parole boards provide no reasons when they deny a parole application—the prisoner is left without any idea of why his application has been turned down. Few courts have considered this particular issue, but the Supreme Court of New Jersey has ruled that a parole board must give reasons for denying parole in order to promote prisoner rehabilitation, honesty and openness in administrative activity, and proper judicial review. The court noted that "the Board's actions are always judicially reviewable for arbitrariness," that state statutes set up definite criteria for parole grant or denial, and that all administrative agencies are required to make "suitable expression of the controlling findings or reasons." The court concluded that such a "course as a general matter would serve the acknowledged interests of procedural fairness and . . . as a suitable and significant discipline on the Board's exercise of its wide powers."[1]

In a somewhat related case, the Supreme Court of California has ruled that California parole officials must discontinue their policy of refusing parole to all persons who sold narcotics for profit, regardless of their good behavior and rehabilitation after incarceration. The court stated:

> A policy that all prisoners who have sold narcotics purely for profit should be retained in prison for the maximum period permitted under the Indeterminate Sentence Law completely disregards the individual prisoner's conduct in prison and his disposition toward reform. If the Authority has in fact adopted such a policy, alteration of the term of imprisonment cannot be used to reward a prisoner for good behavior or to punish him for improper behavior. Neither can it be used to encourage participation in rehabilitative programs designed to prepare an inmate for his return to the outside world. . . . If every offender in a like legal category receives identical punishment, prisoners do not receive individualized consideration. Such a policy violates the spirit and frustrates the purposes of the Indeterminate Sentence Law and the parole system.[2]

Do prisoners have a right to due process at parole hearings?

Theoretically yes, but hearings before the parole board are for the most part meaningless exercises. The prisoner is not represented by counsel or any other advisor, and he has no opportunity to present information favorable to him or to effectively rebut possibly damaging information in his file. In effect, he merely has an interview with the board of parole, or an individual member, which will rarely offer an effective opportunity for the prisoner to present any material that could effect the decision of the board.

The vast majority of courts have rejected complaints by prisoners that parole was wrongfully denied. However, where a prisoner can prove that parole was denied arbitrarily, or that the board failed to give full and fair consideration to the parole application, the courts might intervene. Thus, the Fifth Circuit Court of Appeals has ruled that a prisoner must be given a court hearing on his claim that the parole board relied solely on his prior criminal record in denying parole.[2a]

Procedural rights are almost nonexistent at parole hearings. Even those courts that have provided for assistance of counsel at parole *revocation* hearings have refused to extend such rights to the parole-granting process.[3] The reason usually given by the courts is that parole is a matter of grace or privilege, not a right and therefore may be granted or denied at the complete discretion of the state.

In every real sense, the decision on parole application is based on factors which are the same as those which are determinative at the time of sentencing and recommitment for parole violators. The basic right that must be established in the parole-granting process, therefore, is the right to a fair hearing, and in particular, the right to counsel. If "insight," "evidence of constructive change," and "stability" are the factors upon which the board relies, counsel should be provided to assist an applicant in demonstrating that he meets these criteria. Explanations of extenuating circumstances concerning the original offense and any alleged misconduct in prison, the indications of rehabilitation and self-corrective measures while awaiting sentence or in custody, the development of a probation or parole plan including employment and housing, and plans for medical and psychological treatment and supervision are all more persuasively and adequately set forth by an attorney.

The discretion of the parole board is so great and the standards applied to determine release so vague and ambiguous that a lay prisoner is at a serious disadvantage in presenting his own parole application.

Further, a prisoner should have the right to rebut any adverse information in the institutional report and to present affirmative witnesses and evidence.

Are there restrictions on parolees?

Yes, the rights of persons on parole are greatly restricted. Typically, the parolee must report regularly to his parole officer; he must obtain permission to change his residence or job, or to get married; and he must not have "questionable associates." In addition, many states restrict the parolee's right to travel and to speak freely, and they subject him, his residence, and possessions to searches without a warrant. Failure to comply with any condition of parole may trigger parole revocation and a return to custody. And, of course, any conviction for a new crime while on parole will result in revocation. Approximately thirty-five to forty percent of all those paroled are eventually returned to prison, and many of these parole violators are returned not for commission of a new crime; rather, they are recommitted for violating a condition of parole. Thus the nature of the conditions of parole are of the utmost significance.

Do parolees have First Amendment rights?

Yes. Although courts have traditionally refused to interfere with the administrative rules and regulations of parole boards, in the First Amendment area they have abandoned the hands-off policy and have struck down arbitrary and unconstitutional parole regulations. In an important First Amendment case, a federal district court has ruled that a United States parole board decision to restrict the right of Leon Sobell, on parole for espionage, to travel and speak at a dinner sponsored by a Communist Party newspaper and to participate in anti-war demonstrations was unconstitutional.[4] The court held that First Amendment rights of parolees may be limited only to serve valid penological purposes, and ruled that there had been no showing of any public danger from Sobell's speech, or of any indication that his rehabilitation might be impaired. The court noted that totalitarian states use "rehabilitation" as a means of thought control and that rehabilitation is probably best approached by avoiding degrading and distrustful restrictions.

A California federal district court has similarly upheld the First Amendment rights of parolees in a case where the parolee was required to obtain permission from his parole officer before giving any public speech.[5] On two occasions, the parole officer refused the parolee permission

to speak at colleges about conditions in the state's
prisons, and the court found that on neither occasion had
the parole officer shown a clear and present danger of riot
or disorder. The court, therefore, enjoined the parole
authorities from conditioning parole on a parolee's seeking
advance permission to address public gatherings.

These cases were followed by the decision of the Tenth
Circuit Court of Appeals which struck down parole conditions prohibiting a convicted income-tax violator from
expressing his "fanatical" opinions about the constitu-
tionality of the federal tax laws. The court held that the
parolee had a constitutional right to express his opinions,
but could be prohibited from urging others to violate the
law.[6]

Do parolees have a right to privacy?

The parolee's right to privacy is often circumscribed by
parole regulations which permit parole officers to inspect
a parolee's premises and possessions at any time without
a search or arrest warrant. Obviously, arbitrary intrusions
of privacy result from these restrictions on privacy, but
most courts, stating that parole is both a privilege and a
kind of custody, have held that the parolee cannot complain of Fourth Amendment violations when his right to
privacy and personal autonomy is subject to arbitrary parole practices. In 1970, the Supreme Court of California
held that in parole revocation proceedings, the Adult Authority could consider evidence that may have been seized
in violation of the Fourth or Fifth Amendments, although
that evidence would be excluded at a criminal trial. The
court limited the application of the exclusionary rule[7] to
trials and stated that a parole agency whose delicate duty
is to decide when a convicted offender can be safely al-

lowed to return and to remain in society is in a different posture than the court which decides his original guilt.[8]

Similarly, the Second Circuit Court of Appeals has ruled that the exclusionary rule should not apply at parole-revocation hearings. The court stated that "a parole revocation proceeding is concerned not only with protecting society, but also, and most importantly, with rehabilitating and restoring to useful lives those placed in the custody of the Parole Board. To apply the exclusionary rule to parole revocation proceedings would tend to obstruct the parole system in accomplishing its remedial purposes."[9]

Some courts have established constitutional protections for the parolee. In one case, a federal district court in New York has held that a parolee does not sacrifice his Fourth Amendment right to privacy by agreeing to be released on parole. Law-enforcement officials had illegally seized evidence from the parolee's residence and had started prosecution. The court suppressed the evidence stating that a parolee cannot "generally be stripped of his constitutional rights, particularly since the effect of such a holding would be to expose him to self-incrimination and to surrender of his privacy with respect to matters and offenses other than violation of parole."[10]

It seems apparent that at this point the courts are not willing to grant parolees that quantum of privacy that the Fourth Amendment guarantees to everyone else. However, arbitrary searches or invasions of privacy that are intended only to harass the parolee are not likely to pass muster even under the prevailing judicial attitudes.

For what reasons may parole be revoked?

Parole revocation proceedings may be instituted for any violation of the conditions of parole. The majority of revocations result from convictions for offenses committed while on parole. These are usually termed direct violations of parole and invariably result in a return to prison for the period of time that the parole was intended to cover. Thus the prisoner who is released on ten years' parole will be recommitted on a direct violation to serve the entire ten years, even though his new offense may have been committed with only one year or six months left to the parole period.

A substantial number of revocations are the result of technical violations, that is, a violation of one or more of the conditions of parole. If revocation results under these circumstances, many states provide that the prisoner is entitled to credit for his good "street time," thus limiting the new imprisonment to the time left on parole at the point of violation.

Is a parolee entitled to a revocation hearing?

Yes. Courts have been consistent in requiring hearings on parole revocations and most states have by statute or regulation provided for a revocation hearing, particularly where there is an alleged technical violation. Until June, 1972, however, the parolee was generally not allowed to confront the witnesses against him, or to present evidence on his or her own behalf. The hearing was, in reality, a *pro-forma* proceeding which provided no real opportunity to the parolee to present his side of the case.

In *Morrisey* v. *Brewer*[11] the United States Supreme Court ruled that a parolee was entitled to a parole revocation hearing and mandated that the parolee be given written notice of the charge against him, an opportunity to confront and cross-examine witnesses, the right to present evidence in his own behalf, and the right to a neutral

hearing officer. However, the court left undecided the
question of whether parolees were entitled to the assistance
of counsel.

The court recognized the importance of parole revocation hearings to parolees, stating:

> The liberty of a parolee enables him to do a wide
> range of things open to persons who have never been
> convicted of any crime. . . . Subject to the conditions
> of his parole, he can be gainfully employed and is
> free to be with family and friends and to form the
> other enduring attachments of normal life. . . . He may
> have been on parole for a number of years and may
> be living a relatively normal life at the time he is
> faced with revocation. The parolee has relied on at
> least an implicit promise that parole will be revoked
> only if he fails to live up to the parole conditions. In
> many cases the parolee faces lengthy incarceration
> if his parole is revoked.
>
> We see, therefore, that the liberty of a parolee,
> although indeterminate, includes many of the core
> values of unqualified liberty and its termination in-
> flicts a "grievous loss" on the parolee and often on
> others. It is hardly useful any longer to try to deal
> with this problem in terms of whether the parolee's
> liberty is a "right" or a "privilege." By whatever
> name, the liberty is valuable and must be seen as
> within the protection of the Fourteenth Amendment.[12]

The lower courts are divided on the issue of right to
counsel at revocation hearings. In *Mempa v. Rhay*[13] the
United States Supreme Court ruled that a probationer was
constitutionally entitled to counsel at probation revocation
or deferred sentencing proceedings. Realistically, there are

no differences between parole revocation and probation revocation proceedings since they both involve the basic question of whether a person already convicted of a crime should be given liberty or imprisonment.

The Court of Appeals for the Second Circuit has held that constitutional due process requires that parolees have a right to counsel at parole revocation hearings that may result in their reimprisonment.[14] The court first found that the parolee had a substantial interest in the conditional liberty he enjoyed—revocation would result in that case in eleven years imprisonment, decreased chances of re-parole, and the added stigma of further wrongdoing. Second, the court reasoned that a lawyer, while unable to assist in the discretionary judgments involved in parole revocation, would help the parole board establish and interpret the relevant facts by providing investigation and a sense of balance to the reports. Finally, it was decided that a lawyer's presence would neither delay nor disrupt the functioning of the parole system nor convert the proceedings into an adversary hearing, since the board has the power to structure the proceedings so as to limit potential for disruption.

Similar decisions have been handed down by state courts in New York,[15] Pennsylvania,[16] and Michigan[17] and federal district courts in Wisconsin, California and Florida.[18] Courts which have held that parolees are not entitled to counsel at these proceedings include the Third,[19] Sixth,[20] and Tenth Circuit Courts of Appeals.[21]

NOTES

1. *Monks v. State Board of Parole*, 58 N.J. 238, 277 A.2d 193 (1971). But see *Madden v. New Jersey State Parole*

Bd., 438 F.2d 1189 (3rd Cir. 1971) (No constitutional requirement for statement of reasons for denying parole).

2. *In re Minnis*, 1 Prison L. Rptr. 289 (Cal. Sup. Ct., July 21, 1972).

2a. *Scarpa v. United States Bd. of Parole*, 1 Prison L. Rptr. 213, _____ F.2d _____ (5th Cir. 1972).

3. See, e.g., *Menechino v. Oswald*, 430 F.2d 403 (2nd Cir. 1970).

4. *Sobel v. Reed*, 327 F.Supp. 1294 (S.D. N.Y. 1971).

5. *Hyland v. Procunier*, 311 F.Supp. 749 (N.D. Calif. 1970).

6. *Porth v. Templar*, 453 F.2d 330 (10th Cir. 1971).

7. The exclusionary rule refers to that method used by courts to exclude from criminal proceedings any evidence (such as a confession or contraband) obtained by law-enforcement officials in violation of the defendant's constitutional rights.

8. *In re Martinez*, 83 Cal. Rptr. 382, 463 P.2d 734 (1970).

9. *United States ex rel. Sperling v. Fitzpatrick*, 426 F.2d 1161 (2nd Cir. 1970).

10. *United States v. Lewis*, 274 F.Supp. 184, 190 (S.D. N.Y. 1967).

11. 408 *U.S.* 471 (1972).

12. *Id.* at 482.

13. 389 U.S. 128 (1967).

14. *United States ex rel. Bey v. Connecticut State Board of Parole*, 443 F.2d 1079 (2nd Cir. 1971).

15. *People ex rel. Menechino v. Warden*, 27 N.Y. 2d 376 (1971).

16. *Commonwealth v. Tinson*, 433 Pa. 328 (1969).

17. *Warren v. Michigan Parole Board*, 23 Misc. App. 754, 179 N.W. 2d 664.

18. *Goolsby v. Gagnon*, 322 F.Supp. 460 (E.D. Wis. 1971); *Mozingo v. Craven*, 341 F.Supp. 296 (C.D. Cal. 1972); *Cottle v. Wainwright*, 338 F.Supp. 819 (M.D. Fla. 1972).

19. *United States ex rel. Halprin v. Parker*, 418 F.2d 313 (3rd Cir. 1969).

20. *Rose v. Haskins*, 388 F.2d 91 (6th Cir. 1968).

21. *Williams v. Patterson*, 389 F.2d 374 (10th Cir. 1968).

X

Remedies and Procedure

Vindication of even the most fundamental rights requires an ability to cope with complex court procedures and obscure legal doctrines. No matter how illegal the actions or policies of prison officials may be, protection of rights by our judicial system requires at least some adherence to established procedure and remedies. Various judicial remedies are available to prisoners and specific procedures should be followed to secure them.

Are there any administrative procedures for review of prisoners' complaints?

Yes. Many prisons provide for internal review of complaints registered by prisoners. According to these procedures, a prisoner who wishes to complain about a certain condition of his imprisonment, whether it be medical care, correspondence rights, or transfers to other institutions, may appeal his case to higher officials in the prison.

In practice, however, this is only a "paper remedy." Prison officials rarely change general policy or decisions

117

affecting an individual prisoner in response to a complaint
filed by a prisoner. Moreover, appeals by prisoners to prison
officials to reverse decisions made by lower-echelon personnel such as prison guards almost always fall upon deaf
ears. In fact, not only will the complaint or appeal surely
be denied, but it is not uncommon (although certainly
illegal) for prison officials to punish prisoners merely because they voiced dissatisfaction.

**Is it necessary for a prisoner to have an attorney to
challenge prison conditions in court?**

Not necessary but helpful, for not only can the prisoner
be assured that the routine aspects of litigation will be
handled properly, but suits filed by attorneys will normally
be heard and decided more expeditiously. *Pro se* suits
(that is, suits filed by prisoners) are often totally ignored
by the courts, dismissed without any consideration of
their allegations, or decided, if at all, without benefit of
pre-trial discovery, hearings, or legal argument by the
prisoner. Prisoners do not have a right to appear personally
in court to present evidence or argue their case. Thousands
of *pro se* petitions are filed each year and only a very few
are even considered, much less favorably decided for the
prisoner. It is true that courts will occasionally appoint
lawyers in suits where "important" issues are raised, but
prisoners have no constitutional right to representation in
prisoner rights' cases. And while courts will not usually
dismiss prisoner suits for the failure to meet some purely
technical rules of pleadings that might be required if
lawyers were involved, this small concession usually does
not provide anything more than a foot in the door of the
courts.

Over the past several years, an increasing number of lawyers and legal organizations have taken an interest in prisoner-rights' litigation and, if possible, contact should be made with them to secure legal assistance. (A list of these organizations appears in the Appendix.)

Assuming, however, that the prisoner must file a petition unaided by counsel, there are several general rules which should govern his actions. The discussion will begin with a consideration of the procedures that should be followed by state prisoners. The special problems facing federal prisoners will be discussed in turn.

Should a suit be filed in state or federal court?

Historically, the federal courts have provided far greater protection for those who allege denial of their constitutional rights than have state tribunals. This is particularly true in prisoner rights' litigation where, except for a handful of state court decisions, whatever progress has been achieved has resulted from suits in federal court. Fortunately, the attitude of some state courts seems to be changing, thus requiring some thought on the question of where to sue.

On what basis may prisoners sue in state court?

Access to federal courts for state prisoners is provided by the Federal Civil Rights Act of 1871 which allows for suits against state officials, in federal court, where any "right, privilege, or immunity secured by the Constitution or laws" has been denied to any person.[1] This statute has been liberally interpreted by the Supreme Court and is *the* basis on which suits by prisoners should be initiated wherever a prisoner's constitutional rights are at issue and suit is to be filed in federal court. The prisoner need not apply for any relief from the prison administration or the state courts before suing in federal court under this act. In legal terms, he need not "exhaust state remedies."[1a]

What relief may a prisoner request in suits under the Civil Rights Act?

Under the Civil Rights Act, a prisoner may sue for money damages or for what is legally termed "injunctive" and "declaratory" relief.

When can prisoners expect to be awarded money damages?

Money damages are very rarely awarded, and only where there is a strong showing of the most serious violation of basic constitutional rights and proof of intentional misconduct on the part of prison officials. Recently Martin Sostre was successful in winning damages of $9,300 from the warden of his prison for confinement in segregation of 372 days which had been imposed in retaliation for his political beliefs, black militancy, his past prison litigation, and his threat to sue over prison censorship.[2]

Another case, arising in Mississippi, in which money damages were awarded also points up the extraordinary circumstances which are needed to support such relief. In that case a young man, who was being held pre-trial in a Mississippi jail for petty larceny, was shot by a trustee at the jail and was blinded. The court found that the trustee was grossly negligent, that the shooting was

entirely unprovoked, and held that the superintendent of
the prison was responsible for not exercising due care in
selecting this trustee. Under these circumstances the court
awarded the prisoner eighty-five thousand dollars.[8]

When should a prisoner seek an injunction?

When the prisoner is primarily interested in changing
conditions in the prison, challenging a particular rule,
regulation, or prison policy, or seeking changes in treatment, an injunction should be sought. This can be illus-
trated by a few examples. Let us assume that Prison X
has unconstitutionally restricted access to the courts by
censoring prisoner writs prior to sending them to the
courts. The prisoner should, in his petition, allege the basic
facts and ask the court to enjoin this practice. If successful,
the court will order the prison to cease the censorship involved and to send all writs to the courts without prior
prison review.

Similarly, where a prisoner is punished for exercising
a constitutional right, for example where he is placed in
solitary for filing suit against prison officials, the suit in
federal court should ask not only that the punishment be
enjoined, but also that the court declare that the practice
of punishing prisoners as retaliation for filing suits is unconstitutional. Most prisoner rights' suits filed in federal
court are of this type.

Do prisoners have any remedies in state court?

Yes. State courts, at least in theory, provide a wide
range of remedies to prisoners who suffer from illegal

treatment. All states provide for injunctive suits, similar to those a prisoner might bring under the Federal Civil Rights Act, which can be initiated to secure changes in prison procedures and conditions, whether the rights in question be of a constitutional nature or are created by state statute or regulation. Thus, where a state has established prisoner rights in areas that go beyond what may be required by the Constitution, the prisoner may sue for injunctive relief in state court to secure whatever rights are provided by the state law. This approach is best suited to complaints concerning the physical conditions and personnel of the prison. Some states have detailed codes concerning these matters, including rules pertaining to cell space, medical care, food, exercise, and sanitation. Where prisons fail to meet the standards set out in these codes, suit in the state courts may be advised.

State courts have shown increasing concern in the past several years over the conditions that exist in prisons and jails, particularly where the institutions are used to incarcerate persons sentenced by these courts. As noted in the chapters on cruel and unusual punishment and pretrial detention, state courts have responded affirmatively to complaints in many cities where overcrowding and dangerous and wretched conditions prevail. They have issued injunctions against certain unconstitutional practices and in some cases have gone further in either requiring prison officials to prepare new rules and regulations for the prison or in issuing these regulations by order of the court. Where conditions in local jails or prisons are typically poor, strong consideration should be given to filing the suit in a local state court.

Money damage suits may also be initiated in state courts for either the intentional or negligent denial of a prisoner's rights. This type of suit is most appropriate where a prisoner complains of an injury resulting from illegal physical punishment inflicted by guards, lack of medical treatment, or lack of protection from dangerous inmates. The same practical limitations apply here as were discussed with respect to damage suits in federal courts and prisoners should not expect to achieve much in the way of monetary gains in these suits.

Is habeas corpus a good remedy for prisoners?

Yes. Habeas corpus relief is available to state prisoners, initially in state court and then in federal court. Access to the federal court for habeas-corpus relief is extremely limited for state prisoners. The prisoner must first exhaust the state remedies. This legal doctrine in effect requires the prisoner to sue first and appeal in the state courts, and only if the state suit is unsuccessful will the federal court hear the case. In practice, this limitation precludes habeas corpus suits in federal courts by state prisoners principally because the exhaustion of state remedies will usually take years of litigation. Federal prisoners may, of course, directly apply to the federal courts for the writ of habeas corpus. In either situation, the same general rules apply. Habeas corpus traditionally has been the method by which prisoners could test the validity of their confinement. That is, prisoners could challenge their convictions and sentence by way of habeas corpus and, if successful in showing that their confinement resulted from unconstitutional procedures, could gain their freedom. But habeas corpus is not limited to challenging the reasons for the confinement; it may be used also to examine the conditions of confinement.

Are the possible results different depending upon the type of suit?

In essence, whether the suit filed is for an injunction or writ of habeas corpus, the result is likely to be the same. On a habeas corpus petition, the prisoner is technically requesting release from a particular aspect of confinement. The writ says that it is illegal to confine people under those particular conditions. Using the example described above, where a prisoner has been confined in solitary because he has filed a lawsuit critical of prison officials, he or she could sue for a writ of habeas corpus to gain release from solitary. If successful, the result would be the same as that achieved by an injunctive action: release from solitary and a court ruling that the punishment of prisoners for exercising their right to access to the courts is unconstitutional.[4]

In at least one set of circumstances, however, the type of suit may result in different remedies. Where a prisoner attacks the totality of conditions in a prison as constituting cruel and unusual punishment, an injunctive suit will, if successful, result in an order to change the conditions. A petition for a writ of habeas corpus, on the other hand, may result in an order releasing the prisoner (at least from that institution), though it is likely that the court will instead order conditional release: if the illegal conditions are not changed within a certain period of time, release will be ordered.[5]

Do federal prisoners have any additional remedies?

Yes. Federal prisoners may also sue for injunctive and declaratory relief under statutes which give federal courts jurisdiction to hear cases involving federal questions which include prisoner rights' suits based on the Constitution.[6] In addition, money damages for intentional or negligent acts of prison officials resulting in injury to prisoners may be awarded under the Federal Torts Claims Act.[7]

Federal prisoners seeking injunctive relief, however, should first exhaust their administrative remedies. That is, they should request the Federal Bureau of Prisons to provide the relief requested and, after the predictable denial, then file their suit. This rather perfunctory requirement has been insisted upon by some courts before they will consider judicial action.

May prisoners seek a writ of mandamus?

Yes. The writ of mandamus has been made available to prisoners. This writ is a command issued by a court to an administrative, executive, or judicial officer directing the recipient to either perform a task which is part of his or her legal duty, or to restore to the petitioner rights or privileges which have been illegally denied. The courts have relied, to a great extent, on the "hands-off" doctrine in denying relief under this remedy.

Successful petitions requesting writs of mandamus, however, have been filed in both state and federal courts. The Court of Appeals of New York reversed a lower court's dismissal of a petition by a prisoner requesting that the

Commissioner of Corrections be directed to permit the appellant to exercise his freedom of religion.[8] Pursuant to a petition for writ of mandamus, the Fifth Circuit Court of Appeals ordered the warden of the United States Penitentiary in Atlanta to provide Muslims access to a Muslim newspaper on the same basis that other newspapers were permitted.[9]

The ultimate effectiveness of writs of mandamus, as with other remedies in prisoner petitions, will depend largely on the extent of abandonment of the "hands-off" doctrine by the courts. The remedy already appears to be effective in those cases where the complaint of the prisoner concerns a constitutional or statutory right. However, the reluctance of the judicial branch to become involved in the discipline and control of prison institutions may prevent further expansion of the remedy.

NOTES

1. 42 U.S.C. §1983.
1a. *Wilwording v. Swenson*, 404 U.S. 249 (1971); *Rodriguez v. McGinnis*, 456 F.2d 79 (2nd Cir. 1972) (*en banc*).
2. *Sostre v. McGinnis*, 442 F.2d 178 (2nd Cir. 1971).
3. *Roberts v. Williams*, 302 F.Supp. 972 (N.D. Miss. 1969).
4. *Armstrong v. Cardwell*, 457 F.2d 34 (6th Cir. 1972).
5. See, e.g., *Commonwealth ex rel. Bryant v. Hendrick*, 444 Pa. 83 (1971).
6. 28 U.S.C. §1331.
7. *United States v. Muniz*, 374 U.S. 150 (1963); cf. *Logue v. United States*, 1 Prison L. Rptr. 239, 302 _____ F.2d _____ (5th Cir. 1972) (no recovery under Tort Claims Act where federal detentioner died of tuberculosis in *state* jail where he had been placed by a United States Marshall to await trial).
8. *Brown v. McGinnis*, 180 N.E. 2d 791 (New York, 1962).
9. *Walker v. Blackwell*, 411 F.2d 23 (5th Cir. 1969).

Appendix A

The following is a list of some of the legal organizations which are active in Prisoner Right's Litigation:

1. NAACP Legal Defense Fund, 10 Columbus Circle, New York, N.Y.
2. ACLU Prisoners' Rights Project, 1424 16th St. N.W. Washington, D.C. 20036.
3. National Center for Correctional Law, 1705 DeSales St., N.W. Washington, D.C. 20036.
4. National Committee for Prisoners' Rights, 77 West Eagle St., Buffalo, N.Y.
5. National Legal Aid and Defender Association, National Law Office, 1601 Connecticut Ave. N.W., Washington, D.C.
6. Massachusetts Law Reform Institute, 2 Park Square, Boston, Massachusetts.
7. Prison Law Project, 5406 Claremont Ave., Oakland, Calif.
8. Penal Reform Institute, 110 N. Royal, Alexandria, Va.

In addition to these organizations, a growing number of Legal Aid projects, Public Defender offices, local ACLU offices and Law Schools in every part of the country have started prisoner rights' projects. Prisoners should contact the office of the legal organization closest to their institution for legal assistance and information.

Appendix B

SELECTED BIBLIOGRAPHY

1. Goldfarb and Singer, *Redressing Prisoners' Grievances,* 39 Geo. Wash. L. Rev. 185 (1970).

2. Haft and Hermann, *Prisoners' Rights,* Practising Law Institute, 1972 (2 volumes).
3. Hirschkop and Milleman, The Unconstitutionality of Prison Life, 55 Va. L. Rev. 795 (1969).
4. Jacob, *Prison Discipline and Inmates' Rights,* 5 Harv. Civ. Lib. L. Rev. 227 (1970).
5. Note, *Beyond the Ken of the Courts: A Critique of Judicial Refusal to Review the Complaints of Convicts,* 72 Yale L. J. 506 (1963).
6. Note, *Constitutional Limitations on the Conditions of Pre-Trial Confinement,* 79 Yale L. J. 941 (1970).
7. Note, *Prison Mail Censorship and the First Amendment,* 81 Yale L. J. 121 (1971).
8. *The Prison Law Reporter,* A monthly reporter of prisoner rights developments. Available from 15th Floor, Hoge Bldg., Seattle, Washington.
9. *Prisons on Trial: A Symposium on the Changing Law of Corrections,* 21 Buff. L. Rev. 643 (1972).
10. Singer, *Prisoner's Legal Rights: A Bibliography of Cases and Articles,* Warren, Gorham & Lamont, Inc. (1971).
11. Symposium, *The Right to Treatment,* 36 U. Chi. L. Rev. 742 (1969).
12. *Symposium on Prisoners' Rights,* The Journal of Criminal Law, Criminology and Police Science, Vol. 63, No. 2 (1972).
13. *Symposium on Prisoners' Rights,* 16 Vill. L. Rev. No. 6 (1971).

DAVID RUDOVSKY practices law in Philadelphia and is Staff Counsel for the National Emergency Civil Liberties Committee. In the past few years he has become increasingly involved in prisoner litigation and is currently representing inmates of the Philadelphia County Prison System in a court action seeking improvement of prison conditions. Mr. Rudovsky teaches at the University of Pennsylvania School of Law and has published several articles in law journals including one on the rights of the illegitimate.